GUITAR

· FOR ·

ABSOLUTE BEGINNERS

NEW YORK CITY GUITAR SCHOOL

NYC GUITAR SCHOOL
GUITAR FOR ABSOLUTE BEGINNERS

OBJECTIVE: *To learn fundamental skills, concepts and techniques of great guitar players, play songs by heart and establish a strong foundation for further study in any style.*

GUITAR

• FOR •

ABSOLUTE BEGINNERS

Guitar for Absolute Beginners
©2009, 2022 New York City Guitar School
Text © 2009, 2022 by Dan Emery
Illustrations © 2009 Dan Emery
(pages 7-12, 14, 21, 26-27, 50, 52)
Illustrations © 2009 Alia Madden
(pages 13-15, 17-18, 21, 33, 73, 83, 91, 99, 105-106, 110)
All Photographs by Woody Quinn
except page 35 by Dan Emery,
and pages 48-49 and 78-79 and 112 by Samoa Jodha

Published in the United States by Hal Leonard
7777 W Bluemound Rd, Milwaukee, WI 53213

Publisher: Hal Leonard

Editor: Vinnie DeMasi
Copy Editor: Suzanne Bilyeu
Book Designer: Chika Azuma
Song Arrangements by: Rob Adler
Illustrator: Dan Emery and Alia Madden
Photographer: Woody Quinn, Dan Emery, and Samoa Jodha
Printing: Hal Leonard, Winona, MN
ISBN 978-1-70515-244-7
First printing
Printed and Bound in the United States

What is the Fundamental Secret of Playing Guitar Successfully?

PERHAPS YOU WANT TO PLAY GUITAR because you really love music, and you want to be able to make beautiful music yourself. Maybe you want to eventually play music with other people, or write your own songs, or play for your toddler—or perhaps you want to be a rock star! All of these and others are fine reasons to play guitar.

Regardless of your particular motivation, let us recognize the one thing that you MUST do on your way to achieving your goals. **To be a guitar player, you must play guitar!** That's right! If you truly want to play guitar, let us understand right now that you are going to have to pick up your guitar, hold it in your hands and play it to the best of your ability. This is called "practicing," and the more often you practice, the more and the sooner you will realize your goal and desire of being a guitar player.

In your studies at *New York City Guitar School,* you will gain a solid understanding of the habits and techniques necessary for a lifetime of guitar enjoyment and learning. Your teachers will present these powerful ideas to you in a clear and uplifting manner. But as committed and enthusiastic as the teachers at *New York City Guitar School* are, they will not deserve the credit for your progress. The credit will be all yours; playing guitar is in your hands.

If you will only pick up your guitar and play it regularly, then with the aid of your teachers you will soon be amazing yourself. In fact, I think you will be surprised by how easily and comfortably you will learn. To play guitar with confidence and skill, make a deep and powerful commitment right now to the fundamental secret of playing guitar:

To master guitar playing you must play your guitar!

TO MASTER GUITAR PLAYING YOU MUST PLAY YOUR GUITAR!

CLASS

THE FUNDAMENTAL HABITS OF GREAT GUITAR PLAYERS

{ *Identifying strings, frets and fingers; the rest stroke; chord diagrams; D and G chords; proper fretting; planting fingers; strumming the optimum number of strings; how to practice. FOR NEXT WEEK, GET A TUNER. Plus—Great Songs!* }

his is a hands-on lesson, so grab your soon-to-be trusty guitar, sit down and put it right in your lap, with this text on the table, counter or milk crate in front of you. Today you will begin to internalize the habits of a great guitar player!

WHAT IS THIS THING IN MY LAP?

IT IS CALLED A GUITAR. Since you are now a guitar player, you need to know your way around the guitar, just like an astronaut needs to know which button is which in the space shuttle. So let's learn the PARTS OF THE GUITAR. **I know** that you are eager to cut to

the chase and begin playing fun songs—so please read through this section so that you learn the material and you never need to study it again.

Most of the people taking this course have an acoustic guitar at home like the one pictured below. A picture may be worth a thousand words—but actually reaching out and touching something is worth a thousand pictures. So reach out and touch each part of your guitar corresponding to the labeled parts in the pictures below, and clearly recite the name to yourself. If you are playing a classical guitar, it will have nylon strings and no pickguard. If you are playing an electric guitar, it will have some electronic parts and controllers, but the essentials will be the same.

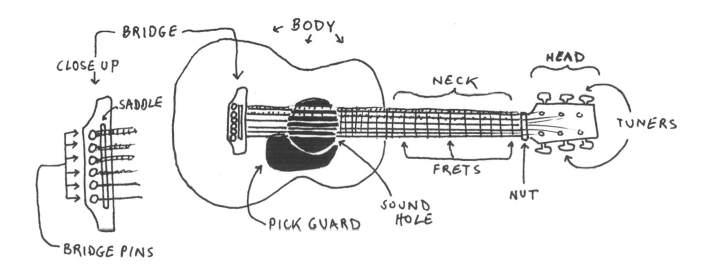

How to Hold the Guitar

WE'RE NOT LEARNING to play classical guitar in this book, and most players in every other style of music rest the guitar on their thigh. Why don't you do that, and play some experimental-having-no-idea-what-you're-doing guitar for a moment. Let your strumming arm rest on top of the guitar, relax, and imagine yourself playing your favorite song. If you feel a little awkward, that is OK, because after all you've been a guitar player for only four or five minutes.

How to Strum the Guitar Correctly

RIGHT NOW you are developing habits that will stay with you for many, many years. Doesn't it make sense to develop good habits immediately? In the next lesson we'll start using a pick, but first we want to achieve perfect, beautiful strumming form, and that is best accomplished by spending some time strumming with your thumb using a technique called "the rest stroke." Let the thumb of your strumming hand (i.e. the right hand for right-handers and left hand for left-handers) rest on the thickest string of the guitar, more or less over the sound hole. Be relaxed—let gravity drag some of the weight of your thumb and hand against the string. Emulate the picture below as much as possible:

Good Guitar Players Strum Efficiently, Using Rest Strokes.

———

When strumming, let your hand drop and brush against the string or strings, coming to a rest against another string or the guitar body.

Now, allow gravity to gently pull your thumb down. It will strum the thickest string as it falls to REST against the next string. Here is a picture of the same thumb after strumming the sixth string with a **rest stroke:**

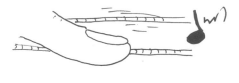

The rest stroke is not only restful and relaxed, but the thumb always comes to a REST on the next string. That's why it is called the rest stroke. Try playing rest strokes on various strings one by one, always with the thumb coming to rest on the next string. When you get to the thinnest string, let your thumb fall against the body of the guitar, as below:

Spend a moment investing in your guitar future by becoming modestly comfortable with rest strokes. Practice playing rest strokes on various strings. Then practice strumming all the strings; your thumb will brush against each string in turn, finishing against the body of the guitar.

By the way, there are two bad habits to especially avoid when strumming: **Don't** grip the bottom of the guitar with your fingers. **Don't** swoop your hand or thumb out into the air. **Do** play smooth, relaxed efficient rest strokes. Using rest strokes is one of the fundamental habits of a great guitar player.

To Play Guitar, You Must Identify Strings. Here's How:

STRINGS ARE NUMBERED from thinnest to thickest —the thinnest string is called the first string, the next thinnest is called the second string, and so on until we get to the thickest string, which is called the sixth string. Remember: **The thinnest string is called the first string.** Learn the string numbers by doing the following exercise—put the thumb of your strumming hand on the sixth (thickest) string and play a rest stroke. Now your thumb is on the fifth string. Play it with a rest stroke. Now find and play the following strings: 4, 3, 2, 1, 6, 1, 5, 2, 3, 4. You now know how to identify strings. Here is a labeled picture:

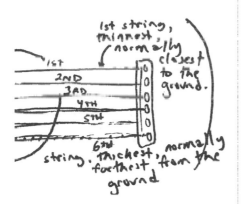

NOTE: THIS IS A NEW, AERIAL VIEW OF THE STRINGS, AS THOUGH THE GUITAR IS SITTING ON YOUR LAP FACING UP.

To Play Guitar, You Must Identify Frets. Here's How:

NOW EXAMINE this pictograph of the very end of the neck, where it meets the head. Note that the frets are also numbered. The fret closest to the nut is called the first fret; the next one is the second fret and so on. Touch the following frets with any finger you like as an exercise: 1, 2, 3, 4, 2, 1, 3.

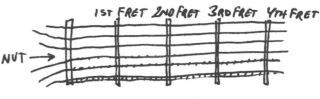

THIS IS AN AERIAL VIEW

Remember, the Thinnest String is the First String and the Thickest String is the Sixth String!

Fret with the Tip of your Finger Almost, but Not Quite, on the Fret!

Do you see what we've accomplished here? We can now identify any intersection of string and fret on the guitar! Try it. Remember that **the thinnest string is the first string** and locate: the first string at the first fret; the second string at the second fret; the sixth string at the third fret; the fourth string at the first fret; the third string at the fourth fret. Again, remember that **the thinnest string is called the first string.** Good work! You now understand how to locate frets and strings.

By the way, since the thinner strings are higher in pitch, they are often called the high strings even though they are closer to the floor. And the thick strings, which are lower in pitch, are called lower strings—even though they are closer to the sky!

Use Your Fingertips to Play Clear and Clean Notes

DID YOU KNOW that fingers might be identified differently when playing different instruments? For example, piano players call their thumb the first finger. But not us guitarists! We call a thumb a thumb, and the index finger is the first finger.

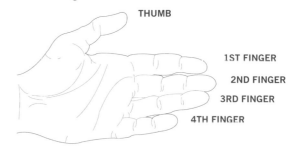

THUMB

1ST FINGER

2ND FINGER

3RD FINGER

4TH FINGER

Now try "fretting" a note. Press the tip of your first finger against the first string just behind the first fret ("behind" means on the head side of the fret, not the body side of the fret). Push down until the string is pressed against the fret. Below is a helpful picture. Notice that this guitarist is really using just the fingertip. Keep your thumb behind the neck, providing support for the fingers; the arm is relaxed with the elbow near the body.

After you fret the first string at the first fret, put the thumb of your right hand on the first string and strum it with a rest stroke. If you hear a buzzing sound, or a "thunk" instead of a clear note, then everything is proceeding normally! Ask yourself, "Am I using the very tip of my finger?" "Is my fingertip close to the first fret (but not actually on top of it)?" "Is my thumb against the back of the neck opposite my first finger?" and "Am I pressing the string down hard enough to press the string against the fret?" Keep trying until you hear your note.

By the way, if your nails are too long, you won't be able to fret clearly. I realize that it really can be a sacrifice to get out the nail clippers and cut them down to size. Just remember that Bonnie Raitt, H.E.R., Taylor Swift and Tracy Chapman cut their nails, and they can play the heck out of the guitar.

Take a moment to fret and strum notes all over the guitar on different strings with different fingertips. Remember to use a beautifully relaxed and efficient rest stroke each time.

Your First Chord

YOU HAVE LEARNED two vital habits of playing guitar—rest strokes and using your fingertips to hold down the string close to the fret. You are now ready to tease the fingers of your fretting hand into a strange configuration known as a "chord." You can think of a chord as a set of notes that sound good together. Your first chord will be the *D major* chord, usually just called "*D*." At first, you may think that *D* stands for "darn it" or "dang it," but soon you will discover that *D* stands for "Dy-no-mite!"

Begin making a *D* chord by putting the first finger of your left hand on the third string at the second fret. This is your **plant** finger. Always when you make a *D* chord, you will begin with this finger, until that time at which all your fingers will fret the chord simultaneously. Of course, I know that you will remember the fundamental good habits of using your fingertips and playing close to the fret. So put the tip of your first finger on that third string almost but not quite on the second fret and press down.

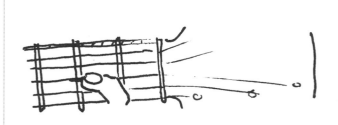

Now in **addition** to your first finger, put your second finger on the first string (thinnest), also at the second fret. Ideally, both fingertips should be close to the fret—it may be helpful to turn your hand slightly to accomplish this.

Finally, reach out with the third finger to play the second string at the third fret. Sort of a reach, huh? Do not be dismayed if this seems difficult—remember that every guitarist had to do this for the first time at some point. Press the strings down with all three fingertips.

You're now making a D chord! Lift all your fingers up and make a D chord again, one finger at a time. Notice that your fingertips outline a triangle.

Then do it again. And again. And again, again, again, again, again.

STRUMMING THE D CHORD

NOW REST THE THUMB of your strumming hand on the fourth string and try an experimental strum or two. Let your thumb fall all the way down to the body of the guitar with each strum.

If each string sounded pristine and clear, you may do a dance of joy. However, if you are like me when I started, or just about everybody else, one, two or even three of the strings made a "buzz" or "thunk" instead of a clear sound. If this is the case, look over at your left hand. Probably one of your fingers is bumping into a string (usually it is the third finger bumping against the first string.)

Here's a chord-troubleshooting checklist:

Are you using your fingertips to fret the chord?
Are you fretting close to (but not on top of) the frets?
Are you pushing the strings against the frets?

Readjust and try again, string by string. Each time you make the D chord, begin with your first fingertip (because it is the plant finger!).

Remember that we seek perfection—but we don't expect it immediately. New guitar players typically need several weeks of practice before their D chord is consistently clear. (But don't wait for perfection—start learning to play songs even if just a couple of strings ring out clearly.)

Please note that ideally, we want to hear not only the three strings that you are holding down with your fingers, but also the fourth string, even though it is open (i.e. unfretted). We DON'T want to hear the fifth and sixth strings— they aren't part of our D chord.

Now, practice making the D chord. The first thing we need to accomplish is a rough familiarity with the chord, so don't worry about how it sounds. Just repeatedly form a D chord by putting the first fingertip down, then the second, then the third, and then a beautiful little strum of the four thinnest strings. Do this for five or 15 minutes, just long enough to begin feeling a little comfortable with the D chord. Then go on to the next section.*

THE *D MAJOR* CHORD
Your journey of a thousand songs begins with D.

ractice Makes Perfect

THE *G MAJOR* CHORD
Knowing G is an absolute must, because it shows up more often and in more songs than any other chord.

*FOR FREE VIDEO LESSONS FROM THIS CHAPTER GO TO
NYCGUITARSCHOOL.COM/BOOKS

Learning to Read Chord Diagrams

There is a conventional way for guitarists to communicate how a chord is fingered, called a CHORD DIAGRAM.

Remember when we zoomed in on the neck of the guitar when we learned how to identify frets? This is an aerial view. We're looking straight down at the guitar. It is lying on its back.

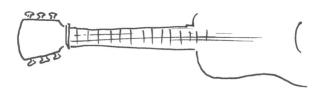

Let's zoom in even more.

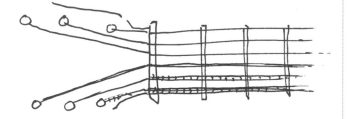

Now let's superimpose the fingertips of a D chord.

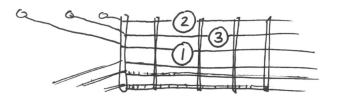

Next, we'll indicate that we're supposed to strum only four strings on this chord by Xing out the strings that we **don't** play (the fifth and sixth strings.) While we're at it, let's make it clear that we **do** play the fourth string, even though we're not fretting it, by placing an "O" for open next to that string.

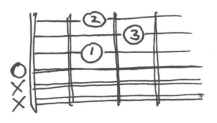

Now, let's turn this picture into a diagram by taking out the head of the guitar, and the extra frets, and by turning the nut and thick strings into just normal lines.

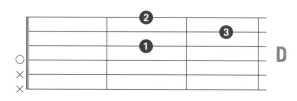

From now on, not only in this course but for the rest of your guitar career, you will be reading and understanding chord diagrams.

(Note: sometimes you'll notice chord diagrams that are drawn vertically, like a tracing of a guitar leaning against the wall.)

The Next Chord: *G Major*

Use your newfound chord-diagram reading skills to learn the *G major* chord. This chord is used more than any other chord in rock and roll.

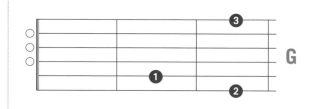

You can think of *G* standing for "giant" because there is a giant stretch involved. Put down the second finger on the sixth (thickest) string, close to the third fret. This is your **plant** finger. Eventually, all your fingers will make the chord simultaneously, but in the meantime, when playing a *G,* lead with the second finger, which holds down the most important note in the chord. Remember to fret with your fingertip close to (but not on top of) the fret.

Then put down the third finger on the opposite side of the guitar neck, on the first (thinnest) string, also close to the third fret.

Finally, put down the first finger on the fifth string (next-to-thickest) and close to the second fret. This is sort of a bonus finger—many competent guitarists leave it off.

Again, as you did with the *D* chord, make a few experimental strums. This time you will strum all six strings. And again, check to avoid those buzzing and thunk-like sounds by asking:

Am I using my fingertips to fret the chord?
Am I fretting close to (but not on top of) the frets?
Am I pushing the strings against the frets?

Take five or ten minutes to achieve a rough familiarity with the *G* chord. Again, we strive for perfection but we don't expect it immediately. Even though your *G* chord doesn't yet sound completely clear, when you are moderately confident with the basic shape of it, go on to the next section.

The Most Powerful Chord Exercise of All

BACK IN MY COLLEGE DAYS, I ran track and cross-country for the University of Idaho. I was always trying to find some special way to practice that would give an extra edge, preferably without running eight or ten miles every morning. Once I read an article about a new workout consisting of jumping on and off a box, and I excitedly ran to see Ken, the trainer. "Ken," I yelled, "I'm gonna jump up on a box and then back down for 45 minutes every morning so that I'll be a better long-distance runner."

Ken looked at me for a moment, then said, "Dan, jumping on and off a big wooden box might help you to become a better box jumper, but if you want to be a better long-distance runner, why don't you go run eight or ten miles?"

So it is with guitar playing. Drills are great, but the best way to get good at playing guitar is to play guitar—so let's begin! The single most powerful thing you can do **right now** to become a better guitar player is to change back and forth between a *D* and a *G* chord incessantly. You see, making a chord isn't the hard part of guitar playing—**changing chords** in the middle of a

song is the hard part. So get ready, and change back and forth between *D* and *G.* Take your time. Remember:

ON THE *D* CHORD

Lead with your first finger . . .
use your fingertips . . . strum four strings.

ON THE *G* CHORD

Lead with your second finger . . .
use your fingertips . . . strum six strings.

It seems to me that most people need to play this change somewhere between 400 and 900 times to feel really confident with it—so do your rock-star guitar-playing self a great favor and change chords relentlessly over the next week! Change chords while listening to music, watching TV, talking on the phone, at breakfast, while riding your unicycle.

Questions and Answers for Beginning Guitarists

Q: *My fingertips hurt—is that okay?*

A: That's okay. As long as they aren't actually bleeding or blistering, there is no problem. Jimi Hendrix, Eric Clapton and Sheryl Crow all had sore fingertips when they started playing guitar! The only way to make your fingertips stop hurting is to play enough for your fingers to toughen up—usually this takes three or four weeks of steady practice. If your fingers do blister, **you might be** practicing too much, but more likely your guitar is in need of adjustment, or you're playing with way too much force, or both. Remember, almost every challenge in guitar is solved with good form, not brute force.

Q: *My wrist hurts—is that okay?*

A: No, that is not okay. Fingertip pain is a pain in a fleshy bit of your finger, which soon adapts. Wrist pain can be in your tendons and joint and can get worse with time. And when pain gets worse, it is hard to practice relentlessly. Avoid wrist pain by keeping your fretting wrist straight, as in the following sketches:

Now, some people may tell you that the bent wrist method is more proper. And there *are* occasions when an experienced guitarist might properly bend their wrist for a particular advanced move, especially if they are seated, with a foot stool, and holding their guitar almost vertically on their laps. But I beg you to avoid bent wrists at this time. If you look at just about any accomplished rock, folk, country, pop or alternative player, and you'll see that their wrists are relatively straight. So let's be like them! In fact, if you have to choose between a clear-sounding chord and a healthy wrist position, be healthy! Chord clarity will come with time and practice. In the unlikely, but not unheard of, event that your wrists, joints or tendons are extremely sore after a week of practice, bring your guitar in so that your teacher can check it for playability, and ask for advice on your playing.

I've included charts and sketches below to help you determine if your pain is okay, or not okay.

DON'T DO THIS—the bent wrist causes wrist pain

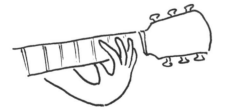

DO THIS—a relatively straight wrist is good.

TYPE OF PAIN	OKAY PAIN	NOT-OKAY PAIN
Fleshy finger pad soreness	👍	
Muscle soreness	👍	
Wrist pain		👎
Joint/tendon pain		👎
Bleeding fingers		👎

I. PRACTICE ACCURATELY.

WHEN YOU PRACTICE playing your guitar, you are literally creating new pathways between the cells in your brain called neurons. As you practice your D chord over and over, for example, you deepen and widen this pathway and make new connections. For the beginning guitarist, a D chord will consist of several different actions in your mind, like this set of commands to your brain and body:

You: "Hey brain and fingers–give me a D chord!"

Your Brain: "OK, let's see here, uh, first I'll put your first finger down on the third string, then I'll, uh, remember that the strings are counted from thin to thick, and then, uh, I'll remember that I need to use the fingertip, OK, now let's go with the second finger—I mean, fingertip—and I'll make sure that the fingertip is close to the fret... so far so good, now for the third fingertip, and I'm not forgetting to keep your fingers coming in all pointy...there you go, a D chord—oh, wait, I almost forgot that I need to have my right hand strum, uh, five, no, four strings!"

It is amazing that we can do this difficult and complex task at all . . . but as you practice and practice, your brain learns the sequence. So after a month of regular practice, your conversation with your brain looks more like this:

You: "Gimme a D!"
Your Brain: BAM! (Your brain has made a D chord and is ready for its next mission.)

Now what can we learn from this insight into how your brain learns to play guitar? Something important, something vital! Since you are using your practice time to create and deepen a sequence of firing synapses, you'd better make sure that the sequence is correct! Otherwise you may end up with several ingrained sequences for your D chord. One of them will be the correct one, and the others will be WRONG. Perhaps you'll put your third finger down on the third string instead of the second string, or maybe you'll make an E chord instead.

The outcome is, according to the researchers, a simple matter of statistics. Let's say that half the time you practice your D chord correctly, a quarter of the time you practice your D chord with the third finger on the wrong string, and the rest of the time you accidentally make an extremely exotic chord, the D major/minor7 chord. Then, after a month of practice, when you are in the middle of playing a song, you'll get this conversation between you and your brain:

You: "Gimme a D!"
Your Brain: BAM! (50% of the time has made a D chord) BAM! (25% of the time has made an incorrectly-fingered D chord) BAM! (25% of the time has fingered a, D major/minor7 chord)

The important thing to remember here is that at this point, it is too late. Your conscious mind has little control over which D you'll get in the middle of a fast song. What you practiced is what you got! That's why it is

Practice Guitar Regularly!

vital that you take the time at the beginning to create an accurate pattern in your mind.

Once you have gradually created the accurate pathway in your mind, you can then go through it quickly, and more quickly, and more quickly again. This idea is expressed by the Latin phrase "Festina Lente," or "Hurry Slowly." If you want to be a fast guitar player then don't worry about being a fast guitar player. Instead, make sure that you are an accurate guitar player, and you will also end up being a fast guitar player. When you want a *D*, you'll get a *D*, and when you want a *D* quickly, you'll get a *D* quickly.

To practice guitar accurately, remember this:

Festina Lente.
When you practice guitar,
practice accurately to create
accurate patterns in your
mind and body.

If Something is Worth Doing, it is Worth Doing Well. Practice with Focus.

2. PRACTICE REGULARLY.

WE ALL HAVE COMPLICATED LIVES. A thousand concerns push and pull us, a hundred desires and duties ask us for our limited time. It can be difficult to find the time or make the time to do even that which we most desire to do–such as practicing guitar. Yet we know that without practicing guitar, we cannot play guitar.

And there is a most effective way for this practice to occur—often! If a person can practice guitar several times over the course of a week, even for a shorter period of time, they will learn more than a person who practices only once in that week, even for a longer period of time. Each time you return to your instrument, it will be with a deeper understanding and a greater ability.

Make a regular time for your guitar practice. Don't go overboard: Set yourself a time and a place that make sense in your life. Some students practice first thing when they get home from work or school. Others practice after dinner. Think of a time and place that will work for you and make a commitment to practice several times a week at least. There may be a time when you don't feel motivated. Don't wait for motivation to strike, but start practicing and the motivation will follow. Of course, if you find yourself playing guitar for hours on end at all times of day and night, that also is OK.

If possible, leave your guitar out of its case on a guitar stand or leaning up against the wall so that it is especially easy to pick up and play. Its purpose is to be played, not to sit in a case!

By making the practice of an art a regular part of your life, you are becoming a practitioner of that art. Be a **practitioner** of guitar. Remember the words of Henry Wadsworth Longfellow:

The heights by great men
**   reached and kept,**
Were not attained by sudden flight.
But they, while their
**   companions slept,**
Were toiling upwards in the night.

3. PRACTICE EFFECTIVELY.

THE GUITAR TEACHER and author David Mead tells a story about a famous classical musician. As a young British man in the 1940s, he was inducted into the National Service. He thought for sure that his music career was ended. But he thought "at least I can try to keep from losing ALL my musical skill and technique." So he made a plan to practice what he considered to be the very most vital elements of music for the short time each day he might get to keep for himself, just to try to stay even.

As the end of his service approached, he found to his surprise that he was a better musician than ever. Those few focused minutes per day were accomplishing more for his technique than hours of practice and playing had done before his enlistment. Why? The answer is this—FOCUS. He spent his limited time doing the very most important things in an intense, focused manner.

Let us do the same. When you sit down to practice, turn the TV off. Put your phone away. Make a plan about what you will practice. And then pay attention to what you are doing! This focus will result in each practice session being as helpful, valuable and fulfilling as possible. As you practice with focus, you will feel great satisfaction in your inexorable progress as a guitarist.

At first, at the beginning of your practice sessions, you may find it difficult to focus. This is normal. Professor Mihaly Csikszentmihalyi of the University of Chicago, has dedicated his life to the study of "flow," which is the state of complete immersion in an activity. He found in his research that to achieve this complete

focus requires an initial effort, perhaps of 15 minutes. For this reason, it is best that you make your practice sessions at least 30 minutes long. For the first half of the session you may find yourself struggling to fully pay attention, and then you may be surprised by how quickly the second half flows by.

As you continue practicing guitar, you will find that it becomes easier and easier to enter this state of complete attention. Merely picking up your guitar and holding it in your lap and hands may become a trigger for relaxed focus.

Remember that old saying *"if something is worth doing, it is worth doing well."* It is worthwhile to play guitar, and it is worthwhile to play it well. Playing well does not mean performing incredible feats of musicianship—it means to play to the best of your ever-expanding ability, and to pay attention to what you are doing.

USE YOUR FINGERTIP TO FRET NOTES, ALMOST, BUT NOT QUITE, ON THE FRET!

Use the very tip of your finger to fret a note; place the fingertip as close to the fret as you can without actually being on the fret.

STRUM EFFICIENTLY, USING REST STROKES.

Let your thumb rest against the thickest string of a chord, then let your hand drop and brush against the strings, coming to a rest against the guitar.

WHEN CHANGING CHORDS, MOVE THE MOST IMPORTANT FINGER FIRST!

For the G move the second finger first; for the D move the first finger first.

ALWAYS PLAY THE OPTIMUM NUMBER OF STRINGS IN A CHORD!

For G strum six strings and for D strum four strings.

REMEMBER THAT THE MOST IMPORTANT HABIT OF A GOOD GUITAR PLAYER IS TO PRACTICE!

PRACTICE SUGGESTIONS FOR CLASS ONE

YOU WILL BE DOING YOURSELF A SERVICE by becoming confident and comfortable with rest strokes and with your first two chords. You don't need to be fast—aim for CONFIDENCE and COMFORT. Practice at least three times for a half hour each. If you practice more, that would be great!

✓ Warm up by making a *D* chord and playing the strings one by one, using rest strokes and striving for clarity on each string. Repeat with the *G* chord. Remember to play the correct number of strings on each chord—four on the *D* and six on the *G*.

✓ Change between *D* and *G* over and over and over, strumming each one in turn. Don't worry about speed or rhythm, but do remember to move the most important finger first (the first finger on *D,* and the second finger on *G*).

✓ Play and sing your songs. Even if you do not consider yourself to be a great vocalist, singing with the songs will greatly improve your guitar playing.

✓ Mess around on the guitar. Fret different notes with different fingers; experiment.

Do Yourself a Giant Favor, and Get a Tuner Now

MY FIRST GUITAR TEACHER, Mike Dulak, said "Dan, I've been playing guitar for 14 years and seven of those years have been spent tuning."

Please, I beg you, don't waste seven years of YOUR life. Do the second-most-useful thing* you can do to ensure your success as a guitar player—GET A TUNER!

When I got married, my wife and I were given two gift certificates by two different friends. One was a $150 gift certificate to a cookware store. The other one was a $150 gift certificate to a music store. I don't know what Miriam did with the first gift certificate, but I ran up to 48th Street (also known as "The Street of 1000 Guitar Shops") and spent the entire $150 on one single state-of-the-art tuner. Now, 25 years later, you can get an even better tuner for free! Where? How? Just go to your favorite app store and search for "guitar tuner" and you'll have lots of great options for a phone-based tuner. You can still buy physical tuners—my favorites are tuners that clip on the the headstock of your guitar, widely popularized by Snark and now made by many companies. Search for "clip on guitar tuner" or drop by your local guitar store.

Don't worry about how to use your new tuning app or clip on tuner yet—we'll cover that in the next lesson!!

* THE FIRST-MOST-USEFUL THING IS TO PRACTICE.

Dear NYC Guitar School Student—

I have written this little note to you from my heart.

You want to play guitar. In fact, you want to play guitar so much that you put your hard-earned money on the line and signed up for a class at New York City Guitar School. *I know you didn't do that lightly, and I don't take it for granted.*

Even more importantly, you made a commitment of your time. As a busy person in New York City, I know how precious your time is. It is difficult to balance work and responsibilities, and still find the time to make your dreams come true.

I have good news for you. At New York City Guitar School, *we have developed what I believe is the world's most effective curriculum for learning to play rock guitar. This curriculum has been created especially for the busy New York City adults who are our students. The lessons have been constantly rewritten and tested on over ten thousand people who have successfully learned to play guitar.*

Furthermore, we have dedicated and expert teachers who give their all to help their students be successful. These skilled coaches have spent years honing their teaching skills and learning guitar pedagogy, and they have taken extensive training in this curriculum. I feel very fortunate to work with them!

But good as our curriculum is, it cannot guarantee that you will play guitar. And as gifted as your teacher may be, he or she cannot make you a guitar player, either. Only one person on this planet can ensure that you learn to play guitar.

That is YOU.

The students who have successfully learned to play guitar in this course practiced three times per week, for a half hour at a time. Some practiced more, but those who practiced three times each week made steady progress. They also attended class regularly. If they had to miss a class, they made it up on another day at one of our NYC locations or in a live video session (you can schedule these make-ups at nycguitarschool.com/members) or reviewed the material in our online video course at nycguitarschool.com/online.

Please take a moment right now to make a commitment to yourself to regular practice and attendance over the next ten weeks. In class ten, when you perform for your classmates or friends, you will be astounded by how much you've learned, and how much fun you've had.

Congratulations on deciding to PLAY GUITAR!

Sincerely,

Dan Emery
Founder, New York City Guitar School

P.S. Please do not hesitate to call **646-485-7244** or email info@nycguitarschool.com with any question!

P.P.S. If you must miss your class, please make it up online at **nycguitarschool.com/members**, or call the school at **646-485-7244** to schedule a make-up class or a discounted private make-up lesson.

P.P.P.S. All in-person or virtual students receive free online access to over 300 videos, exercises, and PDFs. Ask your teacher for a promo code. Students who are using the book to study independently can access free video resources and discounted online courses at **nycguitarschool.com/books**.

Capos and Their Care and Feeding

"Capo" means "head" in Italian. A Mafia capo is the head of a branch of a crime family. Please do not use a Mafia capo to help you play guitar. Instead, use a guitar capo, which is a device that squeezes all six of your guitar strings against whichever fret you place it behind, thus becoming the new "head" of the guitar. It is a tremendously useful tool, because it allows you to leverage just a few chords to be able to play along with lots and lots of different songs.

For example in this lesson, you're learning the incredibly useful D to G progression, which you will use to play the wonderful (and wonderfully repetitive) song **"Sons and Daughters" by The Decemberists.** You could also use those same two chords to play other delightfully beginner-friendly repetitive songs, for example **"You Sexy Thing" by Hot Chocolate.**

If you played and sang both those songs using D and G, you'd sound great and have fun. However if you tried to play along with the recordings of those songs, you'd

Fig. 1a

notice that your D and G would sound in tune with The Decembrists, but out-of-tune with Hot Chocolate. Why? Because Hot Chocolate will not be playing D and G. Hot Chocolate will be playing F and B-*flat* (written by guitarists as $B\flat$, where the lower case "$\flat$" means "flat").

And F and $B\flat$ are not fun chords to play as a beginning guitar player!

But, if you put your capo on the third fret and then you play the D to G you will now be in tune with Hot Chocolate! You see, by putting the capo on the guitar you changed the actual pitch of the notes you were holding down so that a D chord with a capo on the third fret is, strictly speaking, an F chord.

It is of VITAL IMPORTANCE that at this point you do not try to think of such a D chord as an F chord though, because the whole point of a capo is to allow the guitarist to think in terms of the chords he or she knows.

YOU KNOW THE D CHORD. YOU KNOW THE G CHORD. These are the two most important chords you'll ever learn, because they are your first chords. Every future chord will just be another chord.

Surprisingly, you can already play songs with only these two chords. I've listed some below, along with a short-cut approximate chord progression applicable to each one. The way these little charts (which you'll see many of in your guitar career) work is that in each four-beat measure, there is a letter for the chord. For example:

means "Play a *D* chord on the first beat of the first measure, and play a *G* chord on the first beat of the second measure." The ":" symbol means "repeat."

The above chart, on the other hand, means "play *D* on the first beat and *G* on the third beat of the measure."

Often more than one song can be played with the same chords in the same pattern. For example, in this lesson you'll learn **"Sons and Daughters" by The Decembrists.** Remarkably, **"Feel Like Makin' Love" by Bad Company** (open), **"Drive My Car" by The Beatles** (open), **"Walk on The Wild Side" by Lou Reed** (capo X), **"You Sexy Thing" by Hot Chocolate** (capo III) and **"Bells Ring" by Mazzy Star** (capo V) are all also based on the same two-measure pattern:

And as you get faster, smoother and more confident with your D to G you can try something like **"What I Got" by Sublime** (open), which is based on the same change within just one measure:

By the way, **"What I Got"** and lots of other songs can be found in our companion book with Hal Leonard, NYC Guitar School's *Songs For Beginners,* which exactly mirrors this course only with more and different songs. (Visit **halleonard.com** for that and many other songbooks—or search their online portal **sheetmusicplus.com** for "nyc guitar school" for more charts of individual songs graded by class level.)

For each lesson, we've selected songs from different genres. For example, for this lesson we have songs by Oliva Rodrigo, Chuck Berry, and the aforementioned The Decembrists. No matter what song you're playing, start by listening to the recording to get a feel for the song.

A few other notes for your first songs: **"Sons And Daughters"** in particular might feel a bit repetitive—but that is a GOOD thing, because you need lots of practice going from D to G. And when you play **"You Never Can Tell" by Chuck Berry,** take a moment to recognize that you're in great company—John Prine, Bruce Springsteen, Coldplay, Emmylou Harris and others also covered that song.

SONS & DAUGHTERS
PERFORMED BY THE DECEMBERISTS

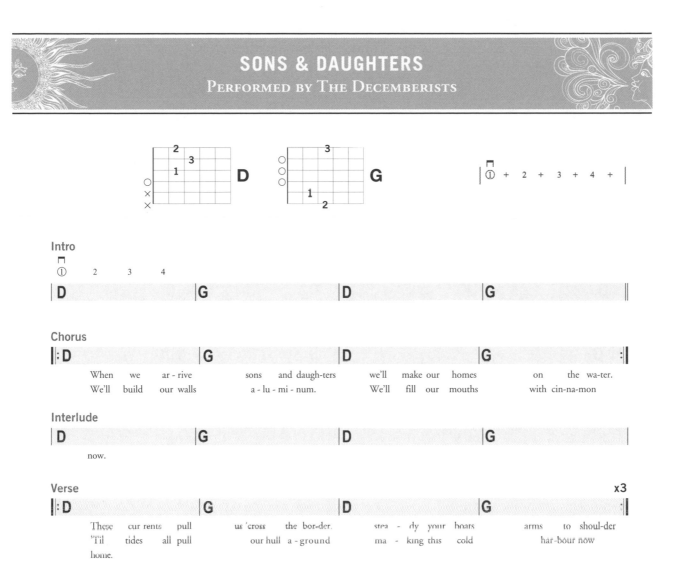

Intro

| D | G | D | G |

Chorus

| D | G | D | G |

When we ar - rive sons and daugh-ters we'll make our homes on the wa-ter.
We'll build our walls a - lu - mi - num. We'll fill our mouths with cin-na-mon

Interlude

| D | G | D | G |

now.

Verse   x3

| D | G | D | G |

These cur-rents pull us 'cross the bor-der. stea - dy your boats arms to shoul-der
'Til tides all pull our hull a - ground ma - king this cold har-bour now
home.

VERSE 2
Take up your arms
Sons and daughters
We will arise from the bunkers
By land, by sea, by dirigible
We'll leave our tracks untraceable now

INTRO

CHORUS

INTERLUDE

CHORUS

INTERLUDE

CHORUS

INTERLUDE

CHORUS

INTERLUDE

OUTRO (INTRO)
Hear all the bombs fade away
Hear all the bombs fade away
Hear all the bombs fade away
Hear all the bombs fade away
Hear all the bombs fade away
Hear all the bombs fade away
Hear all the bombs fade away
Hear all the bombs fade away
Hear all the bombs fade away
Hear all the bombs fade away
Hear all the bombs fade away
Hear all the bombs fade away
Hear all the bombs fade away
Hear all the bombs fade away
Hear all the bombs fade away
Hear all the bombs fade away
Hear all the bombs fade away

DEJA VU
PERFORMED BY OLIVIA RODRIGO

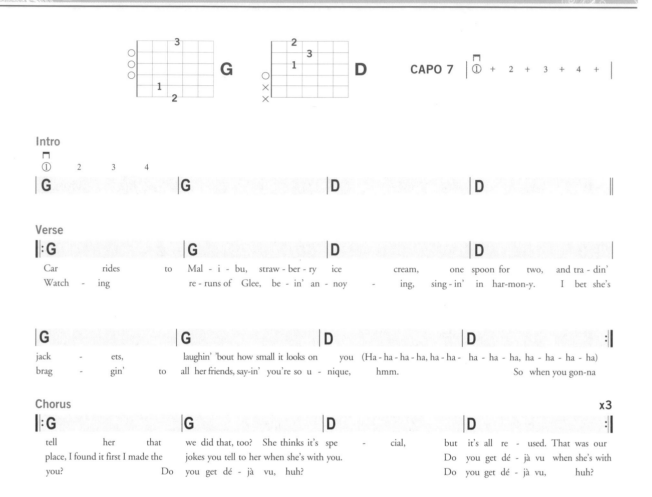

Intro

| G | G | D | D ‖

Verse

‖: G | G | D | D |

Car rides to Mal‑i‑bu, straw‑ber‑ry ice cream, one spoon for two, and tra‑din'
Watch‑ing re‑runs of Glee, be‑in' an‑noy‑ing, sing‑in' in har‑mon‑y. I bet she's

| G | G | D | D :‖

jack‑ets, laughin' 'bout how small it looks on you (Ha‑ha‑ha‑ha, ha‑ha‑ha‑ha‑ha, ha‑ha‑ha‑ha)
brag‑gin' to all her friends, say‑in' you're so u‑nique, hmm. So when you gon‑na

Chorus   x3

‖: G | G | D | D :‖

tell her that we did that, too? She thinks it's spe‑cial, but it's all re‑used. That was our
place, I found it first I made the jokes you tell to her when she's with you. Do you get dé‑jà vu when she's with
you? Do you get dé‑jà vu, huh? Do you get dé‑jà vu, huh?

INTERLUDE (INTRO)

VERSE 2
Do you call her, almost say my name?
'Cause let's be honest, we kinda do sound the same
Another actress, I hate to think that I was just your type
And I bet that she knows Billy Joel, 'cause you played her
    "Uptown Girl"
You're singin' it together, now I bet you even tell her how
    you love her
In between the chorus and the verse

CHORUS

VERSE 3
Strawberry ice cream in Malibu
Don't act like we didn't do that shit, too
You're tradin' jackets like we used to do
    (Yeah, everything is all reused)
Play her piano, but she doesn't know
That I was the one who taught you Billy Joel
A different girl now, but there's nothing new
    (I know you get déjà vu)

OUTRO (INTRO)
I know you get déjà vu
I know you get déjà vu

Deja Vu | Words and Music by Olivia Rodrigo, Daniel Nigro, Jack Antonoff, Taylor Swift and Annie Clark | Copyright © 2021 Sony Music Publishing (US) LLC, Liv Laf Luv, EMI April Music Inc., Daniel Leonard Nigro Music, Ducky Donath Music, Songs Of Universal, Inc., Taylor Swift Music, Hipgnosis Notes and Nail Polish Manifesto | All Rights on behalf of Sony Music Publishing (US) LLC, Liv Laf Luv, EMI April Music Inc., Daniel Leonard Nigro Music and Ducky Donath Music Administered by Sony Music Publishing (US) LLC, 424 Church Street, Suite 1200, Nashville, TN 37219 | All Rights on behalf of Taylor Swift Music Administered by Songs Of Universal, Inc. | All Rights on behalf of Nail Polish Manifesto Administered by Hipgnosis Notes | International Copyright Secured All Rights Reserved | - interpolates "Cruel Summer" (Antonoff/Swift/Clark)

YOU NEVER CAN TELL
PERFORMED BY CHUCK BERRY

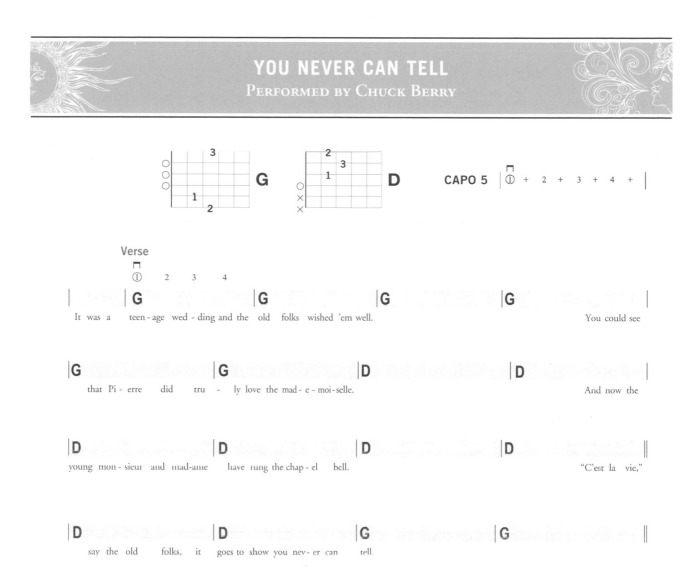

Verse

It was a teen-age wed-ding and the old folks wished 'em well.   You could see

that Pi-erre did tru-ly love the mad-e-moi-selle.   And now the

young mon-sieur and mad-ame have rung the chap-el bell.   "C'est la vie,"

say the old folks, it goes to show you nev-er can tell.

VERSE 2
They furnished off an apartment with
   a two room Roebuck sale
The coolerator was crammed
With TV dinners and ginger ale
But when Pierre found work
The little money comin' worked out well
"C'est la vie," say the old folks
   it goes to show you never can tell

VERSE 3
They had a hi-fi phono, boy
   did they let it blast
Seven hundred little records
   all rock, rhythm and jazz
But when the sun went down
   the rapid tempo of the music fell
"C'est la vie," say the old folks
   it goes to show you never can tell

VERSE 4
They bought a souped up jitney,
   was a cherry red fifty-three
And drove it down to Orleans,
   to celebrate their anniversary
It was there where Pierre was wedded
   to the lovely mademoiselle
"C'est la vie," say the old folks
   it goes to show you never can tell

PIANO SOLO (VERSE)

VERSE 5
They had a teenage wedding
   and the old folks wished them well
You could see that Pierre did truly love
   the mademoiselle
And now the young monsieur and madame
   have rung the chapel bell
"C'est la vie," say the old folks
   it goes to show you never can tell

THE SINGLE MOST IMPORTANT HABIT
OF A GOOD GUITARIST IS PLAYING IN RHYTHM

{ *Using a tuner; playing with a pick; strumming on the beat—quarter-note strums; the A7 chord; how to practice; how to read tablature and play cool licks; memorize songs.* }

OOD GUITARISTS PLAY IN TUNE

THE FIRST THING most guitarists do when they pick up a guitar is to TUNE it using an electronic tuner. I used to be a purist. "I learned how to tune by ear, and so should everybody," I'd say. Then I realized that students who used tuners progressed faster than other students, and even learned to tune by ear better, because they knew what "in-tune" sounded like. Now I think that a tuner is the single most important tool a guitarist can have. As I mentioned earlier, mine cost $150, but technology has advanced so rapidly you can now get a better one for $10-$20, or download an app for free.

To use a tuner, we need to know the names of the strings. A useful mnemonic device is *"Elephants And*

Deers Got Big Ears." This grammatically incorrect statement is true; elephants and deer do have big ears, and the names of the strings from thick to thin are *E-A-D-G-B-E.* Remember—the thickest string is the "Elephant" string, also called the "low *E*" string because it is the lowest, deepest-sounding string. The thinnest string, the "Ears" string, is called the "high *E*" string because it is the highest, brightest-sounding string. See below for several helpful sketches of strings and tuners.

Let's tune! There are two tuner settings, manual and chromatic. Turn yours on or open up your app and if you have a manual tuner, switch it to the *"E/6"* setting. Put your tuner or phone on your leg right next to, or clip your clip-on tuner onto the head of the guitar, and boldly play the sixth string with a rest stroke.

If the note is perfectly in tune, the arrow, pointer, light or other display element will be centered. If the note

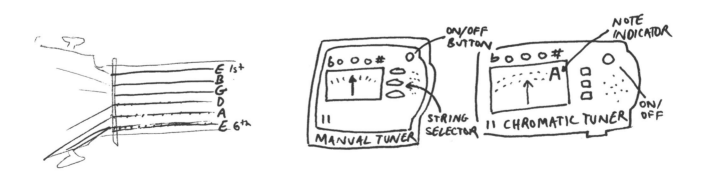

is too low-pitched, the arrow indicator, etc. will point to the left of center. If the note is too high-pitched, the arrow indicator, etc. will point to the right of center. In either case, reach out with your fretting hand, grab the tuner at the end of the sixth string, and turn it. By experimenting you'll soon discover which direction tightens the string, making it higher pitched, and which loosens the string, making it lower pitched. Every so often strum the string again until the display is centered.

Now those of you with chromatic tuners, congratulations! Your chromatic tuner is the bee's knees, and can be used for many arcane tuning needs which you may or may not ever need. Still, there is an extra

step. FIRST you must approximately tune the guitar. When you play that *E* string, ignore the pointer and instead look for the note display, which will tell you what note the string is currently approximately making. If the display says *D* or *E♭* ("♭" is pronounced "flat" and means "a half step lower than") or another note lower than *E*, then you need to tighten the string until the note display says *E*. If the display says *F*, *G♭*, *F♯* ("♯" is pronounced "sharp" and means "a half step higher than") or another note higher than *E* then you need to loosen the string until the note display says *E*. Once the note display says *E*, continue tuning using the centering display.

The Pick

Section 2.3.1. To Pick or Not to Pick

MANY GREAT PLAYERS use only thumbs and fingers to pluck and strum. Most country, rock, folk, pop and punk guitarists use picks. Those who play nylon string (classical) guitars prefer fingers. Fingers are well suited for fingerpicking. Most steel-string players use picks, which rarely blister.

Section 2.3.2. Descriptions

CALLED PICK, PLECTRUM, FLAT PICK. Made of plastic, nylon, tortoiseshell, steel, even felt. Usually teardrop or triangle shaped. Sizes include too big, too small and just right. Thicknesses include really thick, kinda thick, not so thick, thinner than tracing paper. Billy Gibbons of ZZ Top cut up his credit cards and used them as picks.

Section 2.3.3. Holding the Pick

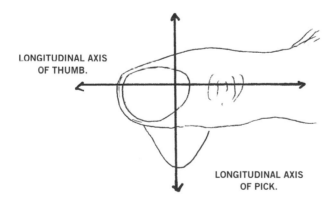

LONGITUDINAL AXIS OF THUMB.

LONGITUDINAL AXIS OF PICK.

Fig. 2a. Relationship of pick to thumb.

Fig. 2b. The crease of the first joint of the first finger is a handy place to tuck a pick.

SECTION 2.3.4. USING THE PICK

Step One: Line up pick with thumb. (See Fig. 2a.)

Step Two: Use index finger to hold pick against thumb. Do not hold too firmly. Do not hold too loosely. Experiment.

Step Three: Strum.

STEP 2.3.5. ADDITIONAL DETAILS

AT FIRST, HOLDING a pick may seem awkward especially when you drop it into the sound hole of your guitar.

The Most Important Element of Guitar Greatness

SO FAR you've been working the PHYSICAL side of playing guitar. You haven't been making much music—you've been teaching your hands to make a *D* and a *G* chord, and you've been internalizing important habits through exercise. These habits include:

• Strumming the correct number of strings in a chord with a beautiful, efficient rest stroke.

• Using the fingertips to fret the strings very close to the fret.

• Planting the most important finger first when changing chords (*D*=1st, *G*=2nd).

Good job! Your *D* and *G* chords give you HARMONY —nice-sounding combinations of notes. But to make music we need more than just harmony. We need RHYTHM! So grab your guitar and read on, because you are about to learn the single most essential skill of a good guitarist—playing in rhythm!

That's right, being "on the beat" is more important than making a nice-sounding chord. Let's perform a thought experiment. Imagine that you're sitting around a campfire with friends, strumming your guitar in perfect rhythm, and everybody's singing along, when suddenly you go to a *G* chord but finger it quite badly. It's more like an X chord—but you keep strumming anyway as though it was a perfect chord.

What happens? Most of your friends don't even notice, that's what! They just keep on drunkenly singing! And afterwards, they refer to you behind your back as "an amazing guitar player." Why? Because you were IN RHYTHM—Job One of any guitarist.

Let's imagine a different scenario. There you are playing next to the campfire, your friends are singing along, you move to that pesky *G* chord and realize that you can't make the change in time. So you **wait to strum** until you've formed the perfect chord, and only then do you strum. What happens now? **Disaster**—everybody gets off rhythm, the song comes crashing to a halt, somebody starts telling a ghost story, and your so-called friends hide your guitar behind some rocks.

From this simple parable, we learn that THE MOST IMPORTANT JOB OF A GUITARIST IS TO PLAY IN RHYTHM! Of course, we want "good chord, good rhythm"—but we also want to know what our priority is. It is rhythm. Let's talk about it.

About 95% of the songs you hear are "in 4," or played with a feeling of four beats. Songs in a feeling of four are usually said to be in 4/4 time, which for right now we can think of as meaning 4 beats at a time, over and over. To get an idea of what I am talking about, tap your foot slowly and evenly, and with each tap of your foot, say a number. This is very important, and we need to be able to do it to play ACTUAL SONGS. Your foot will never speed up or slow down—your voice will be even. Got it? Good, now start slowly, evenly tap your foot, and then begin speaking along:

ONE two three four ONE two three four ONE two three four ONE two three four (etc.)

Do this until you are comfortable and confident with counting and tapping your foot. Remember, no beat is ever faster or slower than any other beat—keep the timing of each beat absolutely even.

STRUMMING IN RHYTHM

NOW THAT YOU KNOW how to tap and count, let's get the guitar involved. You're going to make a *G* chord. You're going to get your right hand ready to strum. You're going to begin tapping your foot slowly and evenly, just as before. You're going to begin counting along slowly and evenly, just as before. But THIS time, in addition to tapping and counting, you will also calmly strum down across all six strings each time that you say a number. This is called "playing on the beat"—and if you can learn to do this, you are destined for success.

So make a *G* chord, start tapping, start counting aloud and start strumming along with every one, two, three and four. Do this several times. (I've written the numbers as numerals instead of words.)

① ② ③ ④ ① ② ③ ④ ① ② ③ ④ ① ② ③ ④

MEASURES AND BARS

IN THIS NEXT SET of "one-two-three-four's," I've divided each set of four beats with a vertical slash. In music, each of these sets of four is called a MEASURE of music. Among the cooler rocker types, a measure is often called a BAR of music. We are those cool rocker types, so we'll usually call those things bars. I'll also put a "*D*" over the top of each bar, to signify that you will be playing *D* chords.

So make a *D* chord, start tapping and counting, and strum on each beat in the following four bars. Do this several times.

D	**D**	**D**	**D**
① ② ③ ④	① ② ③ ④	① ② ③ ④	① ② ③ ④

THIS CHAPTER'S BIG FUN: CHANGING CHORDS IN RHYTHM

YOU ARE JUST A FEW MINUTES AWAY from changing chords in perfect rhythm! To do so, you'll not only need to play in rhythm as you've been doing, but to change chords at the same time. We'll use *D* and *G*. Why don't you prepare by practicing this change for a moment? Remember to lead with the first finger when changing to *D* and the second finger changing to *G*.

Got it? Good. At the end of this paragraph you'll start tapping, you'll start counting aloud, and you'll strum the *D* chord right on the "one." Then **as you continue to** count and tap your foot and strum on each beat, you'll move your fingers into the *G* chord, and strum IT right on the "one" and subsequent beats. Then you'll change back to *D* and strum, then to *G* again, and so on. Do this slowly and evenly and remember that **the strumming hand is most important!** KEEP IT MOVING EVENLY AND STEADILY, even while changing chords. This is called "locking your hand in with the beat."

D	**G**	**D**	**G**
① ② ③ ④	① ② ③ ④	① ② ③ ④	① ② ③ ④

LOCK YOUR HAND IN WITH THE BEAT

THIS MEANS MOVING YOUR HAND exactly with the beat—not rushing, but just confidently letting your hand fall into a strum exactly when each beat falls. It's the single most important skill in rock and roll. It is **much more** important to keep steadily strumming in an even tempo than it is to play a clean-sounding chord.

This is **vital!** If the change is a little too challenging, simply tap your foot more slowly. Spend some time

> The Most Important Job of a Good Guitarist is to STRUM ON THE BEAT!

with this exercise, building skill and confidence. Don't worry too much about how clear the chords sound or even if you are correctly strumming four strings on the *D* and six on the *G*. Although those things are important, let us take care of our first priority—strumming the chord right on the beat.

Take your time. Recall that ideally, you strum four strings on the *D* and six on the *G*—but also recall that a good guitarist always takes care of the most important thing first—and strumming on the beat is the most important thing. Spend five minutes, or 15 minutes, or 50 minutes on this exercise—when you feel confident and consistent, the time is right to move on. (Sometimes students find it helpful to break the chord change into one finger move per beat. On the *D* that would be the first finger, then the second, then the third. On the *G* that would be the second finger, then third, then the first.)

Strumming evenly on each beat is THE essential guitar skill. Even the most advanced rock-star guitarist is often strumming right on the beat exactly as you are doing.

The *A7* Chord

RIGHT NOW, you are the grand master of *D* and *G*. Sadly, there aren't very many songs you can play with only two chords—but with three chords you can play literally thousands. We need one more chord to put those songs in your reach, and here it is—the *A7* chord. Don't worry right now about what the "7" means—just assume it is a lucky number for you. Here is the chord diagram for an *A7* chord. (These things are used so often in guitar that soon you'll be reading them like a pro!)

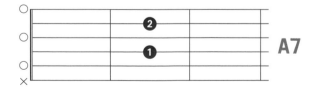

In this chord, the first finger is your plant finger. Once again, become basically familiar with the chord—repeatedly finger the chord, leading with your first finger, and then strum five strings. Occasionally check to hear that each string rings out clearly, asking yourself these very important questions:

Am I using my fingertips to fret the chord?
Am I fretting close to (but not on top of) the frets?
Am I pushing the strings against the frets?

Change chords between the *D* and the *A7*. Don't worry about strumming on every beat at first. Just strum every time you say "one." To remind you to strum just on the one, I've circled each "1" below. Count, tap and play:

D   **A7**   **D**   **A7**
| ① 2 3 4 | ① 2 3 4 | ① 2 3 4 | ① 2 3 4 |

Now let's do this using the single most important skill of any guitarist—playing on every beat. Count slowly, strum evenly. To show you that we are strumming on every beat, I've circled every beat below.

D   **A7**   **D**   **A7**
| ①②③④ | ①②③④ | ①②③④ | ①②③④ |

Repeat these exercises with *G* and *A7*. Remember to lead with your second finger on the *G* and your first finger on the *A7*. Count, tap and play:

G   **A7**   **G**   **A7**
| ① 2 3 4 | ① 2 3 4 | ① 2 3 4 | ① 2 3 4 |

And then:

G   **A7**   **G**   **A7**
| ①②③④ | ①②③④ | ①②③④ | ①②③④ |

How to Read Tablature and Use it to Play Cool Licks

YOU'VE BEEN PLAYING GUITAR for perhaps a week right now, and I'm sure you are constantly wondering "Why can't I play cool licks yet, such as 'Stairway to Heaven,' or the guitar theme to the old TV show 'Batman,' or the lead guitar part from 'Smells Like Teen Spirit' by Nirvana?"

Q: *Dan, what is a lick?*
A: A "lick" is a neat little guitar part, usually made up of single notes. It is called a "lick" because it sounds so tasty.

Now is the time for you to learn the awesome power of tablature and to begin playing lead guitar. Tablature is a system of writing music for the guitar that was developed by flamenco guitarists in 15th-century Spain.

Here is how it works. Do you remember our trusty chord diagram?

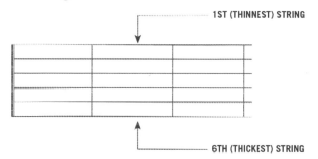

Tablature is based on the same idea; there are six lines, each corresponding to one of the six strings on the guitar. The line at the top stands for the first and thinnest string. The line at the bottom stands for the sixth and thickest string. Just as in a chord diagram, the lines depict an aerial view of the guitar strings, or a tracing of the guitar strings with the head at the left where it says "TAB."

Now to tell you what to play, the person writing tablature will write a number over one of the lines. This number will tell you two things—first, that you should play the indicated string; second, that you should play it at the indicated fret. Read and play through the following examples:

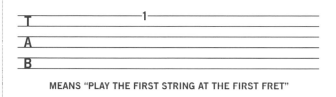

MEANS "PLAY THE FIRST STRING AT THE FIRST FRET"

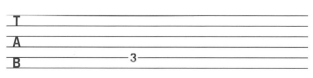

MEANS "PLAY THE FIFTH STRING AT THE THIRD FRET"

When you're supposed to play the string open, without fretting it, the writer will place a zero on the string/line in question. For example:

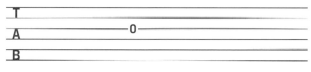

MEANS "PLAY THE THIRD STRING OPEN"

By the way, let's notice something important that tablature doesn't tell us—it **doesn't** say what finger to use! Never think that the numbers in a tab have anything to do with what finger you're supposed to use.

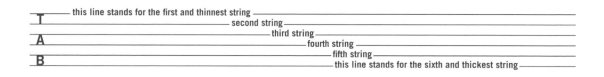

Sometimes more than one string is played at the same time. This is shown by stacking the notes on top of each other. For example:

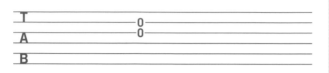

MEANS "PLAY THE SECOND AND THE THIRD STRING OPEN AT THE SAME TIME"

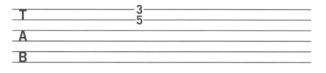

MEANS "PLAY THE FIRST STRING AT THE THIRD FRET AND SECOND STRING AT THE FIFTH FRET AT THE SAME TIME"

Often a complicated-looking tab notation is just telling you to play an open chord! For example:

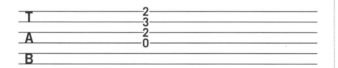

MEANS "PLAY THE *D* CHORD!"

Tablature shows the time element of music by moving left to right—in other words, you first play whatever is written on the left, then you play the next note, then the next and so on.

MEANS "PLAY THE FIRST STRING OPEN, THEN AT THE FIRST FRET, THEN AT THE SECOND, THEN AT THE THIRD"

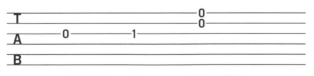

MEANS "PLAY THE THIRD STRING OPEN, THEN AT THE FIRST FRET, THEN PLAY THE FIRST AND SECOND STRINGS OPEN AT THE SAME TIME"

Again, sometimes a complicated-looking tablature is simply a chord written out. For example:

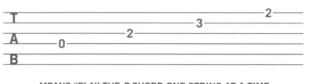

MEANS "PLAY THE *D* CHORD ONE STRING AT A TIME —FIRST THE OPEN FOURTH STRING, THEN THE FRETTED THIRD STRING, THEN THE FRETTED SECOND STRING, AND FINALLY THE FRETTED FIRST STRING"

If you can read and play through all the preceding examples, then you have a great beginning understanding of tablature: Now, it is true that there are lots of other symbols showing techniques such as the "scratch," "slide," "hammer-on," "bend," "vibrato" and so on. You'll gradually be introduced to them. But we won't worry about those right now.

Now you theoretically have the ability to play your favorite songs note for note.

"Note for note" means "exactly as the original artist played it." In many cases, the original artist would never play it exactly the same way twice. Real feeling and understanding are always more important than rote memorization. That said, it's a lot of fun to play something just the way your favorite guitarist did, and it's great for your technique!

Many of your favorite songs have been written out in tablature and are available in book form— many of them produced by our own publisher, Hal Leonard. Furthermore, millions of amateur guitarists have attempted to figure out how to play their favorite songs and have posted their tabs on the Internet. Some of them are quite good. So if you want to play, say, a Coldplay song note for note, you can either purchase the official Coldplay book, which will contain an extremely accurate transcription, or you can search for "Coldplay guitar tab" on the Internet and have your choice of many different tabs of greater or lesser accuracy. Although things change quickly on the Internet, popular tab sites include **ultimate-guitar.com** and **songsterr.com**.

Let me stress though, that good guitar music goes beyond the notes written down on paper. It exists as sound and feeling—so regardless of which tab you might use to figure out how to play your favorite song, it is **vital** and **essential** that you have a copy of the original song to listen to and play along with! So crank up your favorite songs and really **listen** to them before, during and after learning to play a lick or song note for note.

YOUR FIRST COOL LICK WRITTEN OUT IN TABLATURE

SINCE TABLATURE DOESN'T GIVE the proper fingering, I've written the recommended left-hand finger below each note. Since tablature doesn't give pick direction, I've written the recommended right hand picking direction above each note (∏ = down, ∨ = up). Since tablature doesn't give timing, I've also written the timing above each measure.

𝔊ood Guitarists Memorize Songs by Perceiving Patterns in Music!

Usually these patterns are in sets of four!

COOL LICK # 1

THIS LICK is FANTASTIC for teaching your left and right hand to work together. It also is great for teaching your right hand to lock in with the beat, moving down on every beat and up in between beats. Also it is fun to play and fun to listen to. When playing this at a party, don't forget to occasionally yell "Batman!"

Remember your fundamental great habits of playing guitar: Use your fingertips close to the frets. Be efficient—don't let your left-hand fingers get too far away from the guitar. You want a nice, smooth transition between notes, rather than a staccato, pecking-chicken effect. Play slowly and evenly so that you can lock your hand in with the beat.

PRACTICING LICKS

LICKS SHOULD BE PRACTICED AND MASTERED just like chord changes. Go slowly at first, and go correctly. Your fingers and mind are learning important skills as you practice these fancy moves. Gradually build your speed as your confidence and clarity improve.

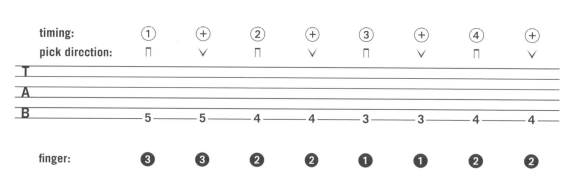

Cool Lick # 1

timing:	①	⊕	②	⊕	③	⊕	④	⊕
pick direction:	∏	∨	∏	∨	∏	∨	∏	∨

```
T |----------------------------------------------------------
A |----------------------------------------------------------
B |----5-----5-----4-----4-----3-----3-----4-----4-----------
```

| finger: | ❸ | ❸ | ❷ | ❷ | ❶ | ❶ | ❷ | ❷ |

MEMORIZE SONGS

DID YOU KNOW that when a professional guitarist plays a five-minute song by heart, he or she has not memorized five minutes of music? That's right—experienced guitar players think of songs in terms of fairly short sections that repeat many times over the course of a song. For example, a typical song arrangement might have a recurring eight-bar verse section alternating with a recurring four-bar chorus section.

Do you think you could memorize the following progression? ("Progression" is a fancier word for a series of chords.)

D   D   D   D   G   G   D   D

Of course you could! Now, do you think you can memorize this next progression?

A7   G   D   D

Take a moment to commit each of these chord progressions to memory. Congratulations! You just learned **"I Still Haven't Found What I'm Looking For" by U2,** among other great songs. Get used to memorizing sets of two, four and eight chords, because nearly every progression in popular music is either two bars, or a multiple of two bars, long.

Class Review

---

1. GOOD GUITARISTS PLAY ON THE BEAT: RHYTHM IS MOST IMPORTANT!

WHEN PLAYING, keep the strumming hand moving in perfect rhythm. This is more important than good fretting, clean changes and accurate strumming. In guitar, as in life, do what is most important, and in guitar that is locking your hand in with the beat!

2. GOOD GUITARISTS PLAY SONGS BY HEART.

TO MEMORIZE SONGS, look for and recognize patterns in the music, especially sets of four and eight.

PRACTICE SUGGESTIONS FOR CLASS TWO

Practice at least three times for half-an-hour each! If you practice more, that would be great!

✓ Warm up by reviewing tablature and playing Cool Lick # 1 incessantly. Take your time—you are not yet striving for speed, but you do want to grow in confidence, clarity and comfort.

✓ Make each of your three chords and strum string by string for clarity.

✓ Play and sing your songs. Memorize them, words and music alike.

✓ Incessantly change chords, when you listen to music or watch TV, leading with the most important finger.

CLASS TWO PROGRESSIONS AND SONG NOTES
D, G, A7

THE 12-MEASURE PROGRESSION below is an extremely common music structure called the 12-bar blues. **"One Good Man"** by **Janis Joplin** and **"Drip Drop"** by **Dion**, which you'll learn in this lesson, follow the 12-bar blues progression. So do thousands of other songs, including **The Beatles'** "Why Don't We Do It In The Road?" (open), **"Tush"** by **ZZ Top** (capo V), **"I Feel Good"** by **James Brown** (open), **"Pride And Joy"** by **Stevie Ray Vaughn** (capo I), **Chuck Berry's** "Johnny B. Goode" (capo VIII), **Jimi Hendrix's** "Red House" (capo VIII), **Van Halen's** "Ice Cream Man" (capo I) and many others.

① ② ③ ④ etc.

:D		D		D		D	
	G		G		D		D	
	A7		G		D		D	:	

Sometimes songs follow the 12-bar blues with a little twist. For example, **"Wipe Out"** by **The Surfaris** is a

PICK
Here's an example of a well held pick.

12-bar blues without chord strums—instead, for most of the song, a single note lead guitar line follows the (implied) chord changes. **"I Still Haven't Found What I'm Looking For"** by **U2** follows a 12-bar blues pattern, except that the first eight bars are repeated before going onto the final four bars.

This week's most challenging song is **"I Fought The Law."** It was written by **Sonny Curtis,** but today it is most associated with The Clash, and you can play along with The Clash using the chart on the following pages. For extra practice, play along with versions by other artists simply by changing where you place your capo. Put your capo on the third fret to play along with Green Day, the seventh fret for Bryan Adams, and the fifth fret to play along with The Bobby Fuller Five, The Stray Cats, Bruce Springsteen, and The Dead Kennedys.

The 12 Bar Blues = Thousands Of Songs

① ② ③ ④ etc.

:D		D		D		D	
	G		G		D		D	
	A7		G		D		D	:|

ONE GOOD MAN
PERFORMED BY JANIS JOPLIN

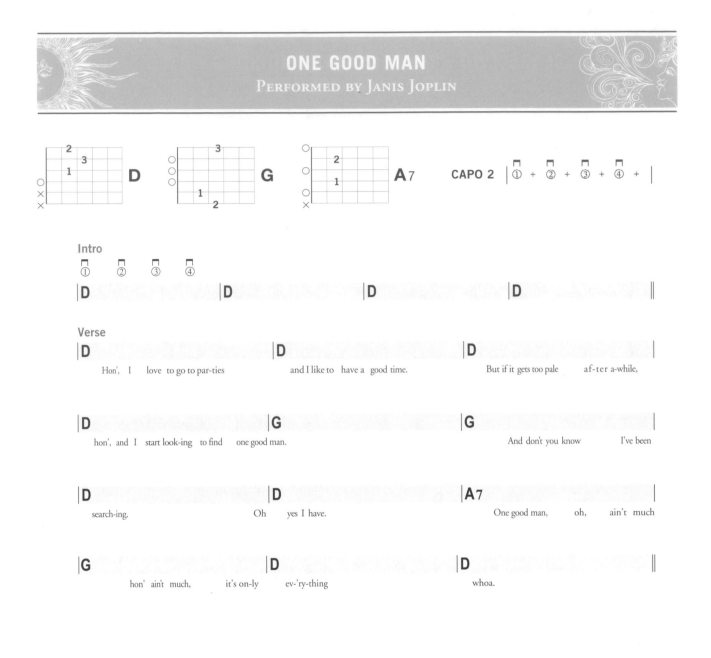

Intro

|D |D |D |D ‖

Verse

|D |D |D |

Hon', I love to go to par-ties and I like to have a good time. But if it gets too pale af-ter a-while,

|D |G |G |

hon', and I start look-ing to find one good man. And don't you know I've been

|D |D |A7 |

search-ing. Oh yes I have. One good man, oh, ain't much

|G |D |D ‖

hon' ain't much, it's on-ly ev-'ry-thing whoa.

VERSE 2
And I don't want much out of life
I never wanted a mansion in the South
I just want to find someone sincere
Who'd treat me like he talks
One good man
Whoa, honey don't you
Know that I've been looking
One good man, ain't much
Hon' it ain't much
It's only everything, whoa

INSTRUMENTAL (VERSE)

VERSE 3
Some girls they want to collect their men
They wear 'em like notches on a gun
Oh honey, but I know better than that
I know that a woman only needs one
One good man
Baby, don't you know I've been looking
One good man
It ain't much, no, no, hon' it ain't much
It's only every little thing, justa everything.

OUTRO (INTRO)

DRIP DROP
PERFORMED BY DION

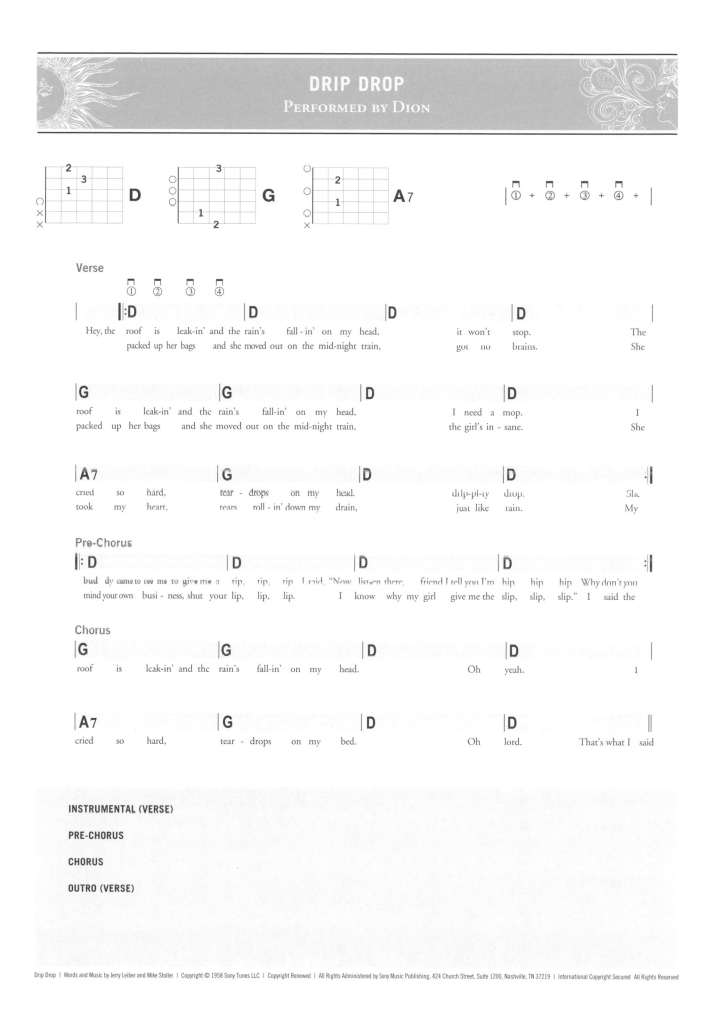

Verse

|: D | D | D | D |

Hey, the roof is leak-in' and the rain's fall-in' on my head, it won't stop. The
packed up her bags and she moved out on the mid-night train, got no brains. She

| G | G | D | D |

roof is leak-in' and the rain's fall-in' on my head, I need a mop. I
packed up her bags and she moved out on the mid-night train, the girl's in-sane. She

| A7 | G | D | D :|

cried so hard, tear-drops on my head. drip-pi-ty drop. She
took my heart, tears roll-in' down my drain, just like rain. My

Pre-Chorus

|: D | D | D | D :|

bud-dy came to see me to give me a tip, tip, tip I said, "Now list-en there, friend I tell you I'm hip hip hip Why don't you
mind your own busi-ness, shut your lip, lip, lip. I know why my girl give me the slip, slip, slip." I said the

Chorus

| G | G | D | D |

roof is leak-in' and the rain's fall-in' on my head. Oh yeah. I

| A7 | G | D | D ‖

cried so hard, tear-drops on my bed. Oh lord. That's what I said

INSTRUMENTAL (VERSE)

PRE-CHORUS

CHORUS

OUTRO (VERSE)

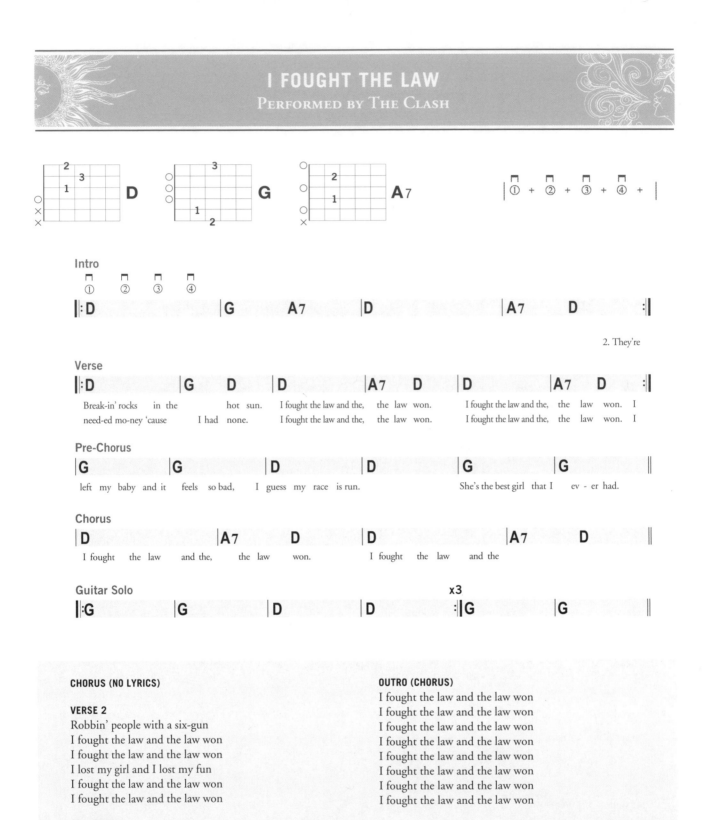

I FOUGHT THE LAW
PERFORMED BY THE CLASH

Intro

|: D | G A7 | D | A7 D :|

2. They're

Verse

|: D | G D | D | A7 D | D | A7 D :|

Break-in' rocks in the hot sun. I fought the law and the, the law won. I fought the law and the, the law won. I

need-ed mo-ney 'cause I had none. I fought the law and the, the law won. I fought the law and the, the law won. I

Pre-Chorus

| G | G | D | D | G | G ||

left my baby and it feels so bad, I guess my race is run. She's the best girl that I ev - er had.

Chorus

| D | A7 D | D | A7 D ||

I fought the law and the, the law won. I fought the law and the

Guitar Solo

x3

|: G | G | D | D :| G | G ||

CHORUS (NO LYRICS)

VERSE 2
Robbin' people with a six-gun
I fought the law and the law won
I fought the law and the law won
I lost my girl and I lost my fun
I fought the law and the law won
I fought the law and the law won

PRE-CHORUS

CHORUS

INSTRUMENTAL (INTRO)

OUTRO (CHORUS)
I fought the law and the law won
I fought the law and the law won
I fought the law and the law won
I fought the law and the law won
I fought the law and the law won
I fought the law and the law won
I fought the law and the law won
I fought the law and the law won

CLASS

Learn This and Learn Many of the Greatest Songs of All Time

{ *Pivot changes and how and why to use them; E minor, C major and D7;* *the concept of progressions; song sections to practice pivot changes.* }

 *:WHAT DO THESE SONGS ALL HAVE IN COMMON?*
"Stay" by Jackson Browne, "Perfect" by Ed Sheerhan, "Love Hurts" by Nazareth, "Every Breath You Take" by The Police, "Crocodile Rock" by Elton John, "Donna" by Richie Valens, "Last Kiss" by Pearl Jam, "Dream" by The Everly Brothers," "Blue Moon" by Elvis Presley, "Stand By Me" by Ben E. King, "Joey" by Concrete Blond, "Crazy" by Aerosmith, "Complicated" by Avril Lavigne, "The Reason" by Hoobastank AND MORE!

A: They are all based, in some fashion, on a single AMAZINGLY POWERFUL chord progression. This happens all the time in music; melodies and lyrics change, but the chords remain the same. A "chord progression" usually refers to a repeating series of chords, and this one goes like this:

G Em C D (or D7)

While we learn this progression, we're also going to learn one of the fundamental habits of a good guitar player—pivoting—which means leaving your fingers down whenever possible. A good guitar player is efficient.

Begin learning to pivot and play all these great songs by making your *G* chord. As always, remember to use your fingertips and play close to the frets.

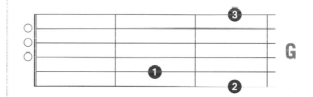

THE *E MINOR* CHORD

Now, PIVOT to an *E minor* chord by LEAVING YOUR FIRST FINGER DOWN. End up in:

Minor chords are usually described as sad-sounding chords. **"The Scientist" by Coldplay, "Hello" by Adele, "Stay With Me" by Sam Smith,** and **"Ain't No Sunshine" by Bill Withers** are examples of songs which begin with a minor chord. Change back and forth between *G* and *Em* until you are comfortable with the change, strumming six strings on each chord, on the first beat. Then, build up to playing on EVERY beat. Remember that good guitarists lock their hands in with the beat. Keep your hand moving even when you are changing chords!

① + ② + ③ + ④ + ① + ② + ③ + ④ +

‖ **G** | **E**m   ‖

THE *C MAJOR* CHORD

THE *C major* CHORD may be a stretch at first—soon it will be one of your favorites. Begin by putting your fingers down in an *E minor.* LEAVE YOUR SECOND FINGER DOWN—it's your PIVOT. Reach out with your third finger, then with your first, to form the *C.*

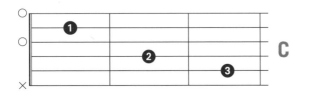

Then go back and forth between *C* and *Em,* pivoting with the second finger. Practice until you feel reasonably confident with this change, playing six strings on the E minor and five on the *C major.*

① + ② + ③ + ④ + ① + ② + ③ + ④ +

‖ **E**m | **C**   ‖

THE *D7* CHORD

A SEVENTH CHORD creates a feeling of motion—the need to travel to some other chord. The *D7* chord, for example, is resolved by a move to a *G* chord. To learn the *D7* chord, begin with a *C* chord. LEAVE THE FIRST FINGER DOWN—it's your PIVOT. Move your second finger and third finger to make the *D7* chord, like so:

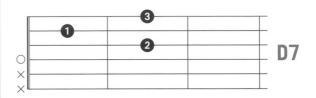

Now make lots of exchanges between *D7* and *C.* Play five strings on *C,* and four on *D7.* When you return to *C* from *D7,* really reach out with that third finger!

① + ② + ③ + ④ + ① + ② + ③ + ④ +

‖ **C** | **D**7   ‖

THE WHOLE SHEBANG*

NOW LET'S DO THE ENTIRE PROGRESSION. Make a *G* and strum six strings. Then PIVOT with the first finger into the *Em* chord and strum six strings. Then PIVOT with the second finger into a *C* chord and play 5 strings. Finally, PIVOT with the first finger into a *D7* chord and play four strings. Then return to a *G* chord by reaching out with your second finger. That's your plant. Now you're ready to begin again!

The Whole Shebang

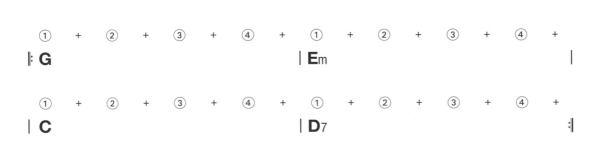

An Important Note about Chord Progressions
Which MUST be Understood to Get the Most from this Class!

SOMETIMES A STUDENT WILL LEARN that they can play a dozen or a thousand songs with the same few chords in the same order, and they will feel a little disappointed. "Oh," they'll say, "there's a trick to this—these songwriters aren't as creative as I thought—they all wrote a song using the same chords."

Q: *Did Picasso use the color blue? Did Picasso, the guy often called the greatest painter of all time, use the color blue? Did he?*
A: Yes, Dan—Picasso, the great painter, did use the color blue.

Q: *But didn't Van Gogh use the color blue, too? Didn't Georgia O' Keeffe use the color blue? Didn't Leonardo da Vinci use the color blue? Are these painters all copycat hacks, copying the color blue off of each other?*
A: They didn't use the color blue because they are copycat hacks. They were all great genius painters, and when you're a painter you use paint, and sometimes paint is blue. It's HOW you paint that makes you a great painter.

Similarly, when you're a songwriter, you use chord progressions. Thousands of songs have been written with the progression "G-Em-C-D", thousands more have been written with the twelve bar "A-A-A-A-D-D-A-A-E-D-A-E", hundreds more have been based on simply "C-F" and so on. The progression isn't what makes a song great—it's the EXPRESSION, the strums, rhythms, tone, technique, attitude, etc. that make a song great.

As a guitar player, you should be attuned to progressions. Usually they will come along in sets of four or eight measures. Constantly be on the lookout for patterns! Now, this doesn't always work, but after many glorious years spent figuring out how to play songs by

listening to CDs and the radio, let me assure you that 99 percent of the songs you want to play contain solid repeating patterns. The more you attune to these patterns, the easier it is going to be for you to understand songs as the songwriter does, and to play songs by heart. So let's always look for patterns in chord progressions.

Now, the fact that this guitar manual is available to order online or to see in a bookstore is literally a dream come true. I'm so glad that working with Hal Leonard allows us to present popular and beloved songs, complete with lyrics and exact guitar parts. But before we had permission to teach exact songs, we made a virtue of the necessity to teach without them. Instead, we taught general chord progressions and strumming which could be used to play many songs.

For example, many songs can be played with only a *D* to *G* chord change, including "**Deja Vu**" by **Oliva Rodrigo** and "**You Never Can Tell**" by **Chuck Berry** (both available in this book), "**What I Got**" by **Sublime** and "**Give Peace A Chance**" by **John Lennon** (both available in our "Songs for Beginners"), or countless more like "**Lively Up Yourself**" by **Bob Marley** or "**Best Day Of My Life**" by **American Authors**. Once you get comfortable with those chords, you will find it an ever easier matter to listen to those songs, and begin playing along, whether you have a chart or not. But at other times the song won't be as obvious. In that case, follow these easy steps:

1. Most importantly, get the song and LISTEN to it. Then try to play along. Often, this will be enough.

2. If you still need help, you may need to get a chart. One way to do this is to search the Internet for "guitar," "chart" and the name of the song and artist

> To Play *with* Heart,
> Play *by* Heart,
> by Noticing
> and Remembering
> Patterns in Music!

you're looking for. You can also purchase an official chart from an online retailer like **sheetmusicplus.com**.

3. Remember, practice makes perfect. Each time you adapt a basic progression to a particular song you will find it easier to play, hear and use.

By the way, here at *New York City Guitar School* we often get calls from people who have played for years, but don't feel as confident as they think they ought to be. Why? Because they don't know any songs, that's why! Imagine—you begin playing guitar because you love songs, and you love the way the guitar sounds in those songs. You learn how to play 10 or 15 chords, and to strum through charts with different rhythms. After a couple of years of this, you walk into a room with a guitar resting in the corner, and you tell the guitar owner, "Hey, I play guitar, too!" "Wow!" exclaims the guitar owner (who is stunningly attractive), "Can you play something for me?" And then you say,

"Well, actually I don't remember how to play anything." Is that what you wanted when you set out to play guitar? Of course not!

This happens to people who never learn to look for and remember the patterns that are found in music. But it won't happen to you, because now and forever more you will remember songs by noticing the repeating four- and eight-measure patterns of which they consist!

Yes, picking out the patterns in music might be a little challenging in the beginning, just like learning a chord is a little challenging—but it is a learned skill and after a while it will become a habit for you. And when you play a song BY heart it is easier to play WITH your heart; it is easier to sing, to feel and to express yourself.

When a student asked the famous jazz guitarist Joe Pass what was the most important thing he could do to improve, he thought he'd be told to "practice scales" or "work on technique"—but Joe Pass told him to learn to play songs by heart, all the way through!

Count and Play in Eighth Notes as You Read Tab and Play a Cool Lick

As YOU KNOW, there are typically four beats per measure of music. That is why when you strum "on the beat" you strum four times per bar. Just as a measure can be divided into four beats, so too a beat can be divided. If we divide it in half, we say that we are playing eighth notes, because we now have a total of eight notes per measure of four beats.

The note that happens "on" the beat is counted as a "one" or a "two" or so on. A note that happens between the beats is counted as an "and" and is said to be "off" the beat.

Here is a great lick which is somewhat reminiscent of the guitar part from "**Peter Gunn**" and which will give all four of your fingers quite a workout. It will also help you to understand counting. Count aloud as you play the lick, and make sure that you play ON all the beats with a DOWN strum as you TAP your foot, and OFF the beats with an UP strum as you LIFT your foot!

Remember to count aloud when you first practice this lick! Understanding rhythm is important, and spending a week counting aloud as you tap your foot will be very helpful to your guitar career. Also remember your fundamental great habits of playing guitar; use your fingertips close to the frets. Be efficient—don't let your left hand fingers get too far away from the guitar. You want a nice, smooth transition between notes, rather than a staccato, pecking-chicken effect. Play slowly and evenly at first!

Somewhat But Not Quite Reminiscent of the Guitar Riff from "Peter Gunn"

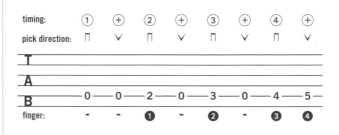

✓ Warm up by playing the lick from a couple of pages back (Somewhat But Not Quite Reminiscent of the Guitar Riff from "Peter Gunn") slowly, accurately and incessantly.

✓ Pivot from *G* to *Em* and back again over and over and over. Do the same thing with *Em* to *C* and with *C* to *D7*. You can sing and play your mini-songs. Every once in a while, strum your chords string by string to check for clarity.

G and *Em:* FIRST FINGER STAYS DOWN
Try singing "**About A Girl**" by Nirvana as you play this change.

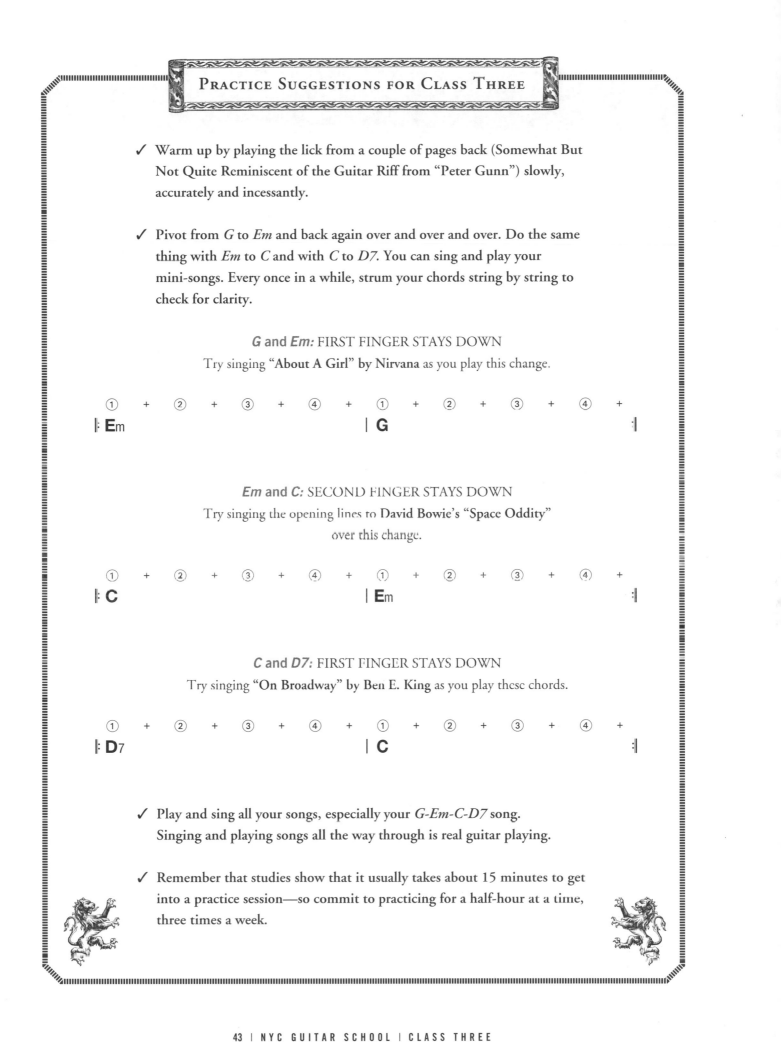

① + ② + ③ + ④ + ① + ② + ③ + ④ +

‖: **E**m | **G**   :‖

Em and *C:* SECOND FINGER STAYS DOWN
Try singing the opening lines to **David Bowie's "Space Oddity"** over this change.

① + ② + ③ + ④ + ① + ② + ③ + ④ +

‖: **C** | **E**m   :‖

C and *D7:* FIRST FINGER STAYS DOWN
Try singing "**On Broadway**" by Ben E. King as you play these chords.

① + ② + ③ + ④ + ① + ② + ③ + ④ +

‖: **D**7 | **C**   :‖

✓ Play and sing all your songs, especially your *G-Em-C-D7* song. Singing and playing songs all the way through is real guitar playing.

✓ Remember that studies show that it usually takes about 15 minutes to get into a practice session—so commit to practicing for a half-hour at a time, three times a week.

CLASS THREE PROGRESSIONS AND SONG NOTES
G, Em, C, D7

THE *E MINOR* CHORD
The first finger is on the same string and same fret in both the Em and G chords, and can be left in place when changing between them.

THE *G-Em-C-D7* CHORD progression is absolutely vital. It is the foundation for hundreds of songs including "**Up On The Roof**" by the **Drifters**, which you'll learn in this lesson and "**Last Kiss**" which was made most popular by **Pearl Jam** (open—and also featured in our companion songbook *Songs For Beginners*). Spend twice as long on each chord and you've got the basis for "**Joey**" by Concrete Blond (open) and "**The Reason**" by Hoobastank (capo IX—but if I were you I would just play it open and sing along—it will sound great). We're going to call this a *One-Six-Four-Five*. Don't worry about why yet—the numbers refer to some simple music theory that we'll cover in a later class. Right now, just concentrate on leaving those pivot fingers down.

One-Six-Four-Five

① ② ③ ④ etc.

‖: **G** |**Em** |**C** |**D**7 :‖

Play the exact same progression only with two chords per measure (two beats per chord) and you'll be strumming **The Marcels'** version of "**Blue Moon**" (open), "**Stay Just A Little Bit Longer**" by Jackson Browne (open), "**Crazy**" by Aerosmith (capo II), and "**Complicated**" by Avril Lavigne (capo X but just play it open). Try out the *One-Six-Four-Five Split Measure* at the top of the next column.

THE *C MAJOR* CHORD
Once you've got the C down, you're well on your way to playing with comfort and confidence.

One-Six-Four-Five Split Measure

① ② ③ ④

‖: **G** **Em** |**C** **D**7 :‖

Here's a common variant of the *G-Em-C-D7* progression heard in songs like "**Beautiful Girls**" by **Sean Kingston**, "**Every Breath You Take**" by The **Police** (capo I) and **Ben E. King's** timeless "**Stand By Me**" (capo II). Notice you're playing the *C* and *D7* for one measure each, but every other chord for two measures consecutively.

THE *D SEVENTH* CHORD
Use the first finger on the second string at the first fret to pivot between C and its good friend, D7.

One-Six-Four-Five Stretched

① ② ③ ④ etc.

‖: **G** |**G** |**Em** |**Em** |
|**C** |**D**7 |**G** |**G** :‖

Play the same progression only beginning with *C* to unlock another of this chapter's songs, "**Rude**" by **Magic!** This pattern is also heard in **Coldplay's** "**Viva la Vida**" (capo I), **Joe Satriani's** "**If I Could Fly**" (capo V) or part of the chorus to **Van Morrison's** "**Brown Eyed Girl**" (open).

Four-Five-One-Six

① ② ③ ④ etc.

‖: **C** |**D**7 |**G** |**Em** :‖

Now it's time to start playing a *G-Em-C-D7* song—or just write your own!

UP ON THE ROOF
PERFORMED BY THE DRIFTERS

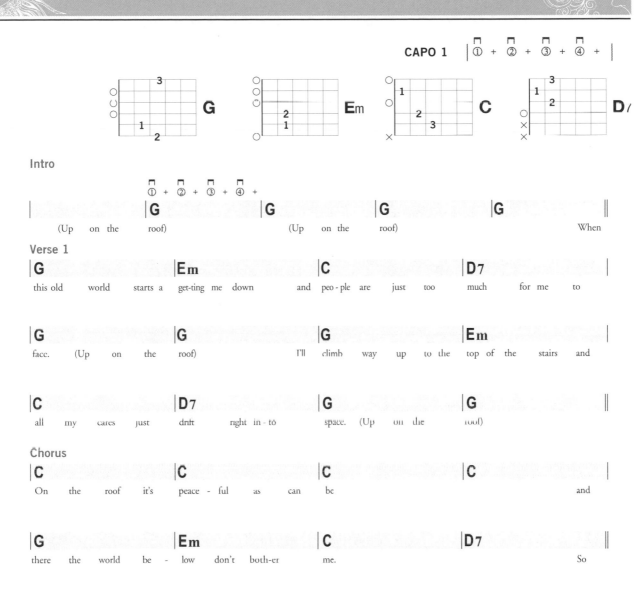

CAPO 1

Intro

| G | G | G | G | |

(Up on the roof)   (Up on the roof)   When

Verse 1

| G | Em | C | D7 | |

this old world starts a get-ting me down and peo-ple are just too much for me to

| G | G | G | Em | |

face. (Up on the roof) I'll climb way up to the top of the stairs and

| C | D7 | G | G | |

all my cares just drift right in-to space. (Up on the roof)

Chorus

| C | C | C | C | |

On the roof it's peace-ful as can be and

| G | Em | C | D7 | |

there the world be - low don't both-er me. So

VERSE 2
When I come home feeling tired and beat
I go up where the air is fresh and sweet
    (Up on the roof)
I get away from the hustlin' crowds
And all that ratrace noise down in the street
    (Up on the roof)

CHORUS
On the roof that's the only place I know
Where you just have to wish to make it so
Up on the roof (Up on the roof)

INSTRUMENTAL (VERSE)

CHORUS
At night, the stars put on a show for free
And, darling, you can share it all with me
I keep-a tellin' you

VERSE 3
Right smack dab in the middle of town
I found a paradise that's trouble-proof
    (Up on the roof)
And if this world starts gettin' you down
There's room enough for two up on the roof
    (Up on the roof)

BEAUTIFUL GIRLS
PERFORMED BY SEAN KINGSTON

CAPO 2

G Em C D7

Chorus

| G | G | Em | Em |

You're way too beau - ti - ful girl, / that's why it'll nev - er work. You'll have me

beau - ti - ful girls, / they on - ly wan - na do you dirt. They'll have you

| C | D7 | G | G |

su - i - cid - al, su - i - ci - dal when you say it's o - ver. Damn all these

su - i - cid - al, su - i - ci - dal when they say it's o - ver. See it

Verse

| G | G | Em | Em |

start - ed at the park, used to chill af - ter dark, oh, when you took my heart, that's when we fell a - part 'cause

say we're too young to to get our - selves sprung, oh, we did - n't care, we made it ver - y clear. And they

| C | D7 | G | G |

we both thought that love would last for - ev - er. (last for - ev - er) They

al - so said that we couldn't last to - ge - ther. (last to - ge - ther) See it's

Pre-Chorus

| G | G | Em | Em |

ver - y de - fined, you're one of a kind, but you mush up my mind, you have to get de - clined. Oh

| C | D7 | G | G |

Lord, my ba - by is driv - ing me cra - zy. You're way too

CHORUS

VERSE 2

It was back in ninety-nine, watchin' movies all the time
Oh, when I went away, for doin' my first crime
And I never thought, that we was gonna see each other
   (See each other)
And then I came out, mami moved me down South
Oh I'm with my girl, who I thought was my world
It came out to be, that she wasn't the girl for me
   (Girl for me)

PRE-CHORUS

CHORUS

VERSE 3

Now we're fussin', and now we're fightin'
Please tell me why, I'm feelin' slighted
And I don't know, how to make it better
   (Make it better)
You're datin' other guys, you're tellin' me lies
Oh, I can't believe, what I'm seein' with my eyes
I'm losin' my mind, and I don't think it's clever
   (Think it's clever)

OUTRO (CHORUS)

You're way too beautiful, girl
That's why it'll never work
You have me suicidal, suicidal, suicidal

RUDE
PERFORMED BY MAGIC!

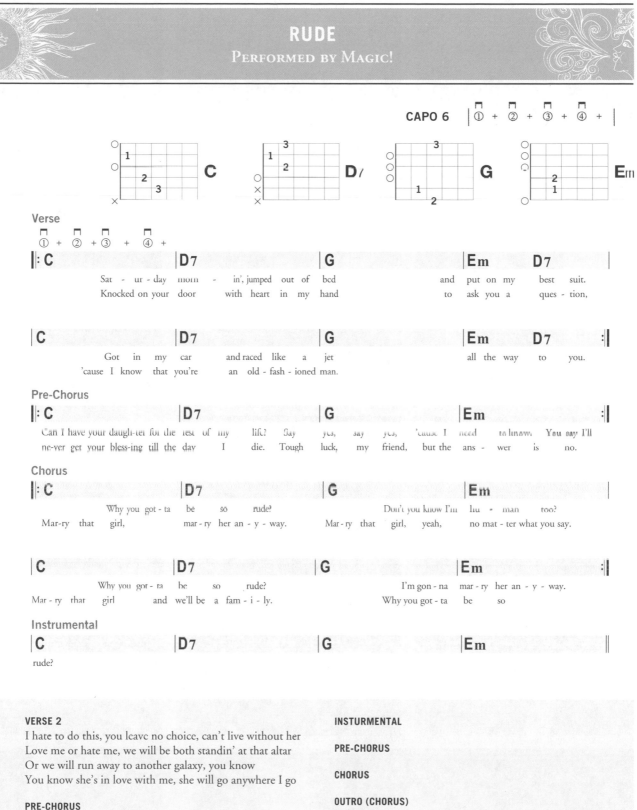

VERSE 2

I hate to do this, you leave no choice, can't live without her
Love me or hate me, we will be both standin' at that altar
Or we will run away to another galaxy, you know
You know she's in love with me, she will go anywhere I go

PRE-CHORUS

CHORUS

INSTURMENTAL

PRE-CHORUS

CHORUS

OUTRO (CHORUS)
Yeah, why you gotta be so rude?
Why you gotta be so rude?

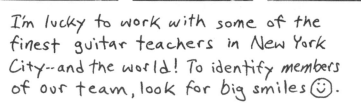

I'm lucky to work with some of the finest guitar teachers in New York City--and the world! To identify members of our team, look for big smiles ☺.

Most of the students pictured on these pages began in the Absolute Beginners class, before graduating to student shows, open mics and NYC stages. Miracles happen when you begin-- and then keep going!

THE SECRET TO PLAYING GREAT RHYTHM GUITAR PLUS THE SMALL BARRE— GATEWAY TO FUTURE GUITAR GREATNESS

{ *Lock your hand with the beat; how to count eighth notes and more licks.* }

OU ARE SMOKING: That's right, you're a smoking ball of guitar fire! You can play *D, G, A7, Em, C* and *D7.* Here's a picture of thousands bowing before you!

Now, let's learn a new rhythm! Right now, you're good at quarter-note strums. They're called that because there are four of them in the typical measure, just like there are four quarters in the typical dollar. And you're good, I hope, at tapping your foot once per beat and strumming down with your hand just as your foot taps down. You are, right?

We can represent this rhythm that you already know like this:

Down	Down	Down	Down
①	②	③	④

Or instead of using the word "down," we could use the official guitarist symbol for down, which is "⊓" = down strum.

So we could rewrite that rhythm like this:

⊓	⊓	⊓	⊓
①	②	③	④

Now, I have a crazy question for you. If you strum down, and then you strum down again, what direction is your hand going **between** those down strums?

If you said "up," then give yourself 25 gold stars, because you are right. What goes all the way down must come up before it can go down again. We guitarists identify the moment when your hand is coming up as being "off the beat." So **on the beat** you strum down, and **off the beat** you lift your hand up to get ready to strum again. There are four beats, so there are four off-beats. This makes a total of eight, so you could describe what we will learn in this lesson as **eighth-note strumming.** Since this involves swinging your hand up and down, we could also call this strum the **swing strum** or **alternate strumming.**

To get the idea of this, let's first **count aloud** as you tap your foot. On the beat, as you tap down, say "one" or whatever the number is. Off the beat, when you lift your foot, say "and," which will be written as "+." Really try to **feel** the beat, as you tap your foot. **Feel** the heaviness of the beat. Do this for several measures in a row, until you're comfortable and confident counting aloud with your foot tap.

You say:	"one"	"and"	"two"	"and"	"three"	"and"	"four"	"and"
The count is:	①	⊕	②	⊕	③	⊕	④	⊕
With your foot:	tap	lift	tap	lift	tap	lift	tap	lift

Now it is time for actual eighth-note strums! Grab your guitar and make a chord—a *G* chord, let's say. Count aloud and tap your foot. Each time you say a number, strum **down**: That's the downbeat. Each time you say "and," strum **up**, that's the upbeat. Above each count I've written the official guitar symbols for down (⊓) and up (∨).

```
⊓   ∨   ⊓   ∨   ⊓   ∨   ⊓   ∨
①   ⊕   ②   ⊕   ③   ⊕   ④   ⊕
| G                                |
```

Don't worry about the exact number of strings you hit with your up strum. You don't need to hit all the strings—just make sure you catch a few. Keep a nice, loose feeling in your arm and hand as you strum. Most importantly, feel the beat. Strum **down, on** the beat, and strum **up, off** the beat.

Play through the measure of eighth notes a few times, until you feel confident and comfortable. This technique is also called alternate strumming because you **alternate between** down and up strums.

Now try the *D* chord.

```
⊓   ∨   ⊓   ∨   ⊓   ∨   ⊓   ∨
①   ⊕   ②   ⊕   ③   ⊕   ④   ⊕
| D                                |
```

This one is a little trickier because it's only 4 strings. But persevere: If Keith Richards learned to do it, so can you!

Understanding ON and OFF the beat is very important. For the rest of your guitar career, you'll be playing extremely complicated alternating strum patterns based on this fundamental precept:

The secret to playing great rhythm guitar is to move your hand with the beat.

Usually this means: ON the beat, strum DOWN and OFF the beat, strum UP.

CHANGING IN RHYTHM

NOW WE'RE GOING TO PLAY this rhythm as we change chords—from an *Em* to a *G,* let's say. We'll discuss this further. But first, give it a try. Count yourself in, tap your foot, and play:

```
⊓ ∨ ⊓ ∨ ⊓ ∨ ⊓ ∨   ⊓ ∨ ⊓ ∨ ⊓ ∨ ⊓ ∨
①⊕②⊕③⊕④⊕   ①⊕②⊕③⊕④⊕
‖:Em              | G              :‖
```

At first, you probably won't be able to make your chord change exactly between the very last up strum of the *G* and the very first down strum of the *Em*.

Good guitar players begin moving to the next chord DURING the "and of four," so that they can cleanly finger the new chord on the next "one." That's taking care of JOB ONE, the most important part of guitar playing—which is playing the chord right on the beat. KEEP YOUR STRUM HAND MOVING no matter what, down on the downbeat and up on the offbeat. Then you change chords AS you strum.

Let's try that change again. I've put three asterisks below the "and of four" to remind you to begin changing chords there.

```
⊓ ∨ ⊓ ∨ ⊓ ∨ ⊓ ∨   ⊓ ∨ ⊓ ∨ ⊓ ∨ ⊓ ∨
①⊕②⊕③⊕④⊕   ①⊕②⊕③⊕④⊕
‖:Em           *** | G           ***:‖
```

Got that? An excellent way to master this rhythm will be to pick a pair of chords and strum your way back and forth between them, before jumping into a song. Here are some nice pairs:

G-Em   Em-C   C-D7   D7-G   D-G   D–A7   G-A7

LET'S LOOK AHEAD in your career as a guitar player. Here you are, learning lots of great chords and great songs, becoming comfortable with your "axe," and playing up a storm. But speaking of storms, there is one lurking out there in the future. It is called the "barre chord," or more often it is called "the @*#^! barre chord!" It is the technique which separates the guitar players from the guitar weenies. Many times in my career as a guitar teacher I have picked up the ringing telephone only to hear a sobbing voice on the other line. With effort I'll be able to make out the words "finger," "pain" and "help, please, help" and I know that yet again someone is calling for assistance with barre chords.

Q: *Dan, what is a barre chord?*
A: A barre chord is a chord in which one finger, usually the first, holds down more than one string at the same time—sometimes even four or five!

I have good news for you—that crying, sobbing, disheartened guitar player pleading for barre chord help will not be you! Why not? Because my fellow teachers at the *New York City Guitar School* and I have discovered that by teaching the "small barre" well ahead of the "big barre" we can ensure that students smoothly and comfortably play barre chords like the complete and natural guitar demigods they are. So even though you won't learn the full barre chord for some time, maybe even a few months, let's lay the foundation right now.

Let's examine the small barre more closely by trying one out. The small barre requires you to hold down two strings, the first and the second, with your first finger. Take your guitar in hand and place your first finger down flat on the first two strings at the first fret, as close to the fret as possible. Here is a helpful picture.

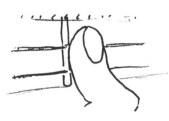

Note that the first finger is locked out at the first joint. Note also that the knuckles of the fretting hand are forward. Try the small barre a few times, and strum each of the strings to make sure that you are holding them down cleanly. Be patient—this usually takes a little practice! The muscle for this technique comes from the palm and the thicker part of your finger, with a little help from your thumb. By the way, I know that one of the fundamental great habits of playing guitar is to use your fingertips but a barre is a different technique. Use the padded part of the end of your first finger, nice and flat.

The best way to practice the small barre is to use it to play famous licks. The small barre appears in countless songs, differing only in the fret where it is played and the rhythm. In fact, a significant percentage of whatever hits happen to be on the radio at this very moment use this move. It is one of the fundamental techniques of a great lead guitar player.

SMALL BARRE LICK # 1

THIS IS A SMALL-BARRE LICK reminiscent of the first single-note guitar line heard in **"Smells Like Teen Spirit" by Nirvana**, and it's a fun way to practice your small barre. Several months from now you'll really need to use a barre for an advanced "big barre chord" and you'll be very happy that you practiced this. So put your first finger down flat on the first and second strings, nice and close to the fret, and try it out. Play down on the second string/first beat, and up on the first string/and of one.

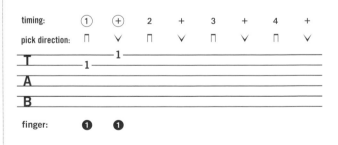

SMALL BARRE LICK # 2

TRY TURNING that guitar line into an exercise. On the first beat you'll pick down and then up on the second string. On the second beat you'll pick down and then up on the first string. And so on!

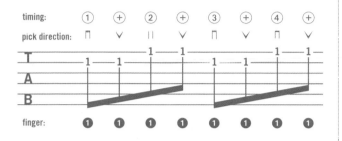

timing:	①	+	②	+	③	+	④	+
pick direction:	⊓	∨	⊓	∨	⊓	∨	⊓	∨

```
T ----------1---1---------1---1--
A --1---1------------1---1--------
B -------------/--------------/---
```

| finger: | ❶ | ❶ | ❶ | ❶ | ❶ | ❶ | ❶ | ❶ |

THE CLASSIC SLIDING SMALL BARRE

THIS LICK has been used in a thousand songs and a half-million solos! I first learned it in "**Johnny B. Goode" by Chuck Berry**. It begins with a slide, which is indicated by the symbol "/". In a slide, you place your finger at one fret and strum, and then you slide your finger to another fret as the first note is still ringing. In this case, begin with a small barre on the fourth fret. Then, as you pick the two strings, slide your small barre to the fifth fret, keeping pressure down on the strings. Then you'll strum the small barre at the fifth fret twice more.

We're going to play this lick with a rhythm called a **triplet**, because there are three notes packed into one beat. We'll need to count this a little differently than

we've counted before. Now we'll say "**one-trip-let-two**-trip-let-**three**-trip-let-**four**-trip-let" to count a full measure. The entire lick is packed into the first beat.

timing:	①	(trip)	(let)	2	trip	let	3	trip	let	4	trip	let
pick direction:	⊓ sl	⊓	⊓									

```
T --4/5---5---5-----------------------------
  --4/5---5---5-----------------------------
A ------------------------------------------
B ------------------------------------------
         ⌐3⌐
```

| finger: | ❶ etc. | | | | | | | | | | | |

Licks are often like chords in that they are set moves that are combined by skilled guitarists in new and expressive ways. Just as many different artists use a *G major* chord in their songs, artists from Odetta and ZZ Top to Metallica and Parry Gripp all use the small barre in their songs.

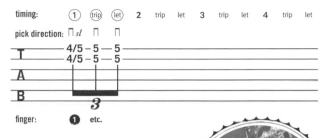

THE SMALL BARRE
Note how flat the first finger is. This move is used constantly in lead guitar solos, plus it is the foundation for barre chords, which will come in very handy in your future guitar career.

One of the most common intro and solo moves in rock is to play the sliding small barre triplet repeatedly. You can hear this move in songs like "**Revolution" by The Beatles** and "**Dust My Broom" by Elmore James**. The slide only takes place on the first beat. On the beats two, three and four just play the small barre with triplet down strokes (two-trip-let, three-trip-let, four-trip-let). Try to smoothly repeat the entire measure four times in a row:

The Classic Sliding Small Barre #2

timing:	①	(trlp)	(let)	②	(trip)	(let)	③	(trip)	(let)	④	(trip)	(let)
pick direction:	⊓ sl	⊓	⊓	⊓	⊓	⊓	⊓	⊓	⊓	⊓	⊓	⊓

```
T --4/5--5--5--6--5--5--5--5--5--5--5--5--
  --4/5--5--5--6--5--5--5--5--5--5--5--5--
A ----------------------------------------
B ----------------------------------------
         ⌐3⌐     ⌐3⌐     ⌐3⌐     ⌐3⌐
```

| finger: | ❶ etc. | | | | | | | | | | | |

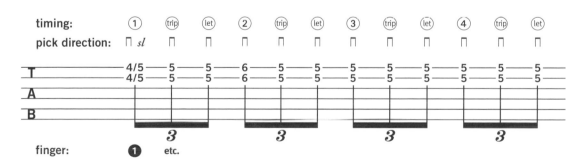

GOOD GUITARISTS KNOW THAT
PLAYING IN RHYTHM IS MOST IMPORTANT!

The secret to playing great rhythm guitar is to move your hand with the beat.
Usually this means: ON the beat, strum DOWN. OFF the beat, strum UP.

Good guitarists are efficient.
LEAVE FINGERS DOWN WHENEVER POSSIBLE
—PIVOT, PIVOT, PIVOT!

USE YOUR FINGERTIP TO FRET NOTES,
ALMOST BUT NOT QUITE ON THE FRET.

STRUM EFFICIENTLY, USING REST STROKES.

WHEN CHANGING CHORDS,
MOVE THE MOST IMPORTANT FINGER FIRST.

ALWAYS PLAY THE OPTIMUM NUMBER OF
STRINGS IN A CHORD.

PERCEIVE AND REMEMBER PATTERNS IN MUSIC!

✓ Warm up by playing your small barre licks. Then play your licks from Classes Two and Three.

✓ Play your Class Four songs incessantly and smoothly and repeatedly. Sing along—download/stream the song if you aren't familiar with the words.

✓ Play all the way through your other songs.

My First Guitar

MANY PEOPLE LEARN TO PLAY guitar on a borrowed instrument. Jimi Hendrix did, and so did I. My first guitar actually belonged to the father of my best friend, Ted, back in the rural North Idaho country where I grew up.

It was perhaps inevitable that Ted and I would become best friends. We had a lot of important qualities in common, including:

1. We were the only two boys in our entire high school class who did not chew tobacco.
2. We were the only two boys in our entire high school class who took physics.
3. Nobody else wanted to be seen with us.

Ted lived on a farm high above the Potlatch River Canyon. His father, Robert, was a thick, strong and frugal farmer of wheat and lentils who rose early each morning for a focused 12 or 14 hours of work in the fields before returning to the house to relax before bedtime with some accounting or minor repair jobs. Ironically, he was allergic to wheat, and during the harvest season I mostly remember him as one big red inflammation. The dual intensity of his allergy and work ethic were matched by his shrewd love of bargains and his careful hoarding of any item that someday might prove useful under some scenario, no matter how unlikely.

(In the close environs of a New York City apartment, such an attitude could prove dangerous. For example, I recently read about a guy in the Bronx who saved everything until one of the narrow passageways through his apartment collapsed, trapping him. Luckily, after several days he was able to reach his phone and call for help. As an industrious farmer living on several hundred acres, Robert did not worry about being trapped by his stockpile of potentially useful items, although he did build several more barns in his spare time.)

Sometimes Robert's bargain hunting came in handy for me. For example, Ted, his brother Jed, my brother Luke and I all shared a love of Coca-Cola. One day, Robert took us all to the supermarket with a stack of coupons for cases of Coca-Cola for some unbelievably low price. He sent us in and out of the store with coupons and five-dollar bills until the car was completely full. When I said, "Uh, where are we going to sit on the way back?" he didn't even bother to answer. He gave each of us teenagers an extra case to carry on the five-mile walk back home. In an effort to lighten our load we drank as many cans as we could, but it made the trip much longer because soon we were forced to stop every 50 yards to relieve ourselves. Also, we had to tie the empty cans up in our shirts because we knew Robert would insist that they be returned for the nickel deposit.

Anyway, I digress, because this story is about my first guitar. The story actually begins a very long time ago, before I was born, when the young man who would become Ted's father saw an unbelievably good deal on a cheap acoustic guitar in a department store that was going out of business. He laid down his 12 dollars and took the guitar home to this conversation with his young wife, which I have made up on account of not being there:

Roz: "Now what did you go and buy that for, Bob? You're never going to use it!"
Robert: "This will come in handy one day. You'll see."

Then Robert carefully placed the guitar in the corner of one of his first barns, along with some other things which might very well come in handy one day, like a coffee can full of bent nails and the driver-side door from a 1934 International one-ton pickup truck.

Years passed. The sun rose and set. The Earth turned from day into night. Each morning, Robert woke up and worked like a force of nature, farming, building and occasionally fathering sons, pausing only to stockpile useful items. Week by week such items were placed in the barn, layer upon layer, like sediments being deposited onto the bottom of a prehistoric sea.

Then, after a long time, I, Dan Emery, was born, mostly grew up, and became extremely interested in becoming a rock star. I had a great band name, which I will not reveal except under medieval torture. I also had a great band—Ted would be the singer, his brother Jed would be the drummer, my brother Luke would be the keyboard player, and I would be the guitar player. (A bass player was deemed unnecessary.) I even had my band's first write-up in the paper thanks to a gullible reporter on a tight deadline.

Clearly, the only thing standing between me and stardom was the fact that I lacked a guitar. Ted and Jed apparently mentioned this at home because one morning they told me that their father not only had a guitar, but he would lend it to me for as long as I wanted, as soon as he found it.

Two months later, I held my first guitar in my hands. The strings were brittle with age, the neck was bowed, and the first time I tried to tune it one of the tuners fell off, but I loved it. I practiced for two hours the first day, two hours the second day, and then I built up from there.

Each time I attempted to tune the guitar, I tightened the strings a little more and the neck of the guitar warped a little more under the tension, until the strings were almost impossible to push down against the frets. One day I heard a creaking sound from the corner of the room where the guitar was leaning. Right before my astonished eyes, the guitar convulsed like a tasered python, and then the neck snapped off with a dramatic crack and twang.

"Ted," I said, "the guitar broke."

"That's no problem," he replied. "We have a shop."

Ted and Jed had been fixing farm equipment since an early age and considered no repair job beyond them. They saw their mission as two-fold: first, to reattach the neck of the guitar to the body, and secondly to render it impervious to future breakage. They put metal plates on the neck and body, then connected them with a thick metal brace on each side of the neck with the same care and attention to durability they used when repairing plows. They even welded it to be sure nothing came loose. When I got the guitar back, there was so much steel plate on it that I had to squat to lift it. Also, it could never be tuned again. It was great, especially since I wanted to play heavy-metal guitar anyway.

In conclusion, I want to publicly thank Robert for giving me my first guitar, and to applaud his foresight in stockpiling it for my future use. If aliens invade, if a gigantic volcanic explosion plunges the world into three years of winter, if there is a major meteor impact, etc., etc., I will immediately depart New York City and head for the barns that contain the solution to any problem that may arise. I will leave you with another imagined conversation between Robert and Roz:

Robert: "I told you that guitar would come in handy one day."
Roz: "Oh, Bob—have another Coke."

You are building up some serious guitar-playing firepower, and you are now ready to learn one of the most mind-blowingly popular chord progressions of all time. Using this progression you can play hundreds or thousands of songs, including: **"Swing, Swing" by The All-American Rejects** (open), **"Don't Matter" by Akon** (capo II), **"Far Away" by Nickelback** (capo IV), **"My Name Is Jonas" by Weezer** (capo IV), **"I'm Goin' Down" by Bruce Springsteen** (capo II) and many others. We'll see much more of this intensely powerful progression in future classes. In the meantime, pick your favorite *G-D-Em-C* song, adjust a capo as needed, and play along with the band.

Remember, keep your strum hand moving!

Mind Blowing Progression in G

Songs will often be driven by the same chords played in the same order, but starting on a different chord in the progression. For example if we play the progression above but simply start on the *E minor* instead of the *G,* we'll be playing the underlying harmony for 90s rock anthems like practically all of **The Cranberries' "Zombie"** (open) and **The Smashing Pumpkins' "Disarm"** (open).

90s Rock Anthem

∏ ∨ ∏ ∨ ∏ ∨ ∏ ∨
①+②+③+④+ etc.

‖**E**m |**C** |**G** |**D**   :‖

In all the excitement of playing *C* chords, do you remember that *A7* chord? I hope so, because here is a classic *D-A7-G-A7* repeating pattern. Please note that the chords change every two beats—that means that for every chord, you'll get a down-up-down-up.

KEEP YOUR HAND MOVING, even when you are changing chords. This pattern can be discerned in songs like **"The First Cut is the Deepest" by Cat Stevens** (you will learn the Sheryl Crow version later on), the verse to **"All Star" by Smash Mouth** (capo IV), most of **"Small Town" by John Cougar** (capo IX) and **"Love Stinks" by the J. Geils Band** (capo X).

FOR FREE VIDEO LESSONS ACCOMPANYING THIS BOOK GO TO NYCGUITARSCHOOL.COM/BOOKS

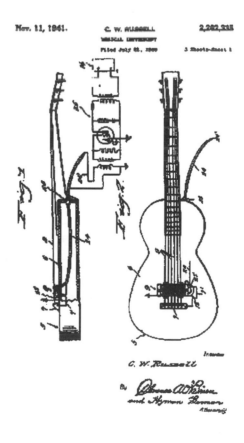

A-PUNK
PERFORMED BY VAMPIRE WEEKEND

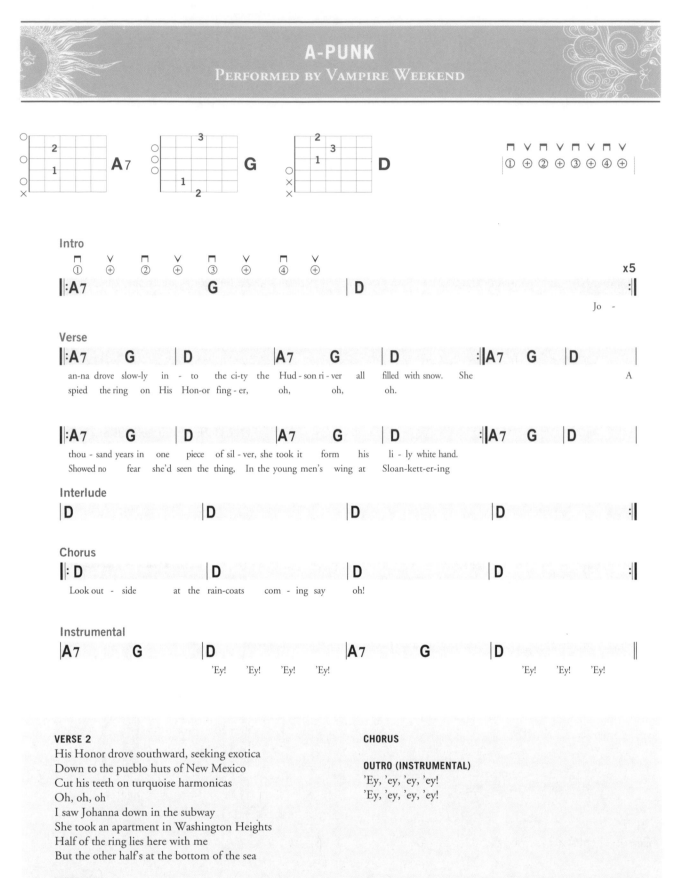

Intro

| A7 | | G | D | x5 |

Jo -

Verse

| A7 | G | D | A7 | G | D | A7 | G | D |

an-na drove slow-ly in - to the ci-ty the Hud-son ri - ver all filled with snow. She   A
spied the ring on His Hon-or fing - er,   oh,   oh,   oh.

| A7 | G | D | A7 | G | D | A7 | G | D |

thou - sand years in one   piece of sil - ver, she took it   form   his   li - ly white hand.
Showed no   fear   she'd seen the thing, In the young men's   wing at   Sloan-kett-er-ing

Interlude

| D | | D | | D | | D | |

Chorus

| D | | D | | D | | D | |

Look out - side   at the rain-coats   com - ing say   oh!

Instrumental

| A7 | G | D | A7 | G | D |

'Ey!   'Ey!   'Ey!   'Ey!   'Ey!   'Ey!   'Ey!

VERSE 2

His Honor drove southward, seeking exotica
Down to the pueblo huts of New Mexico
Cut his teeth on turquoise harmonicas
Oh, oh, oh
I saw Johanna down in the subway
She took an apartment in Washington Heights
Half of the ring lies here with me
But the other half's at the bottom of the sea

INTERLUDE

CHORUS

OUTRO (INSTRUMENTAL)
'Ey, 'ey, 'ey, 'ey!
'Ey, 'ey, 'ey, 'ey!

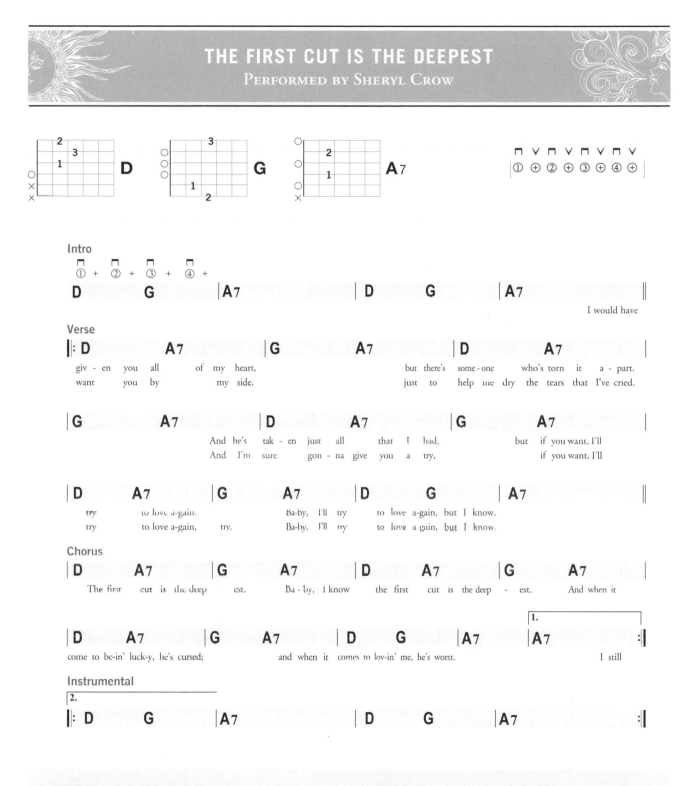

Intro

D G |A7 | D G |A7 ||

I would have

Verse

|: D   A7 |G   A7 |D   A7 |

giv - en you all   of my heart,   but there's some - one   who's torn it a - part.
want   you by   my side,   just to   help me dry the tears that I've cried.

|G   A7 |D   A7 |G   A7 |

And he's tak - en just all   that I had,   but if you want, I'll
And I'm sure   gon - na give you a try,   if you want, I'll

|D A7 |G   A7 |D G |A7 ||

try   to love a-gain.   Ba-by, I'll try   to love a-gain, but I know.
try   to love a-gain,   try.   Ba-by, I'll try   to love a gain, but I know.

Chorus

|D A7 |G   A7 |D A7 |G   A7 |

The first   cut is the deep   est.   Ba - by, I know   the first   cut is the deep - est.   And when it

1.

|D A7 |G   A7 |D G |A7 |A7   :||

come to be-in' luck-y, he's cursed;   and when it comes to lov-in' me, he's worst.   I still

Instrumental

2.

|: D G |A7 | D G |A7   :||

VERSE 3

I still want you by my side
Just to help me dry the tears that I've cried
But I'm sure gonna give you a try
'Cause if you want, I'll try to love again
(Try to love again, try to love again)
Baby, I'll try to love again but I know
Oh-oh

CHORUS

OUTRO (INTRO)
The first cut is the deepest
Baby I know
The first cut is the deepest
Try to love again

SEVEN BRIDGES ROAD
Performed by The Eagles

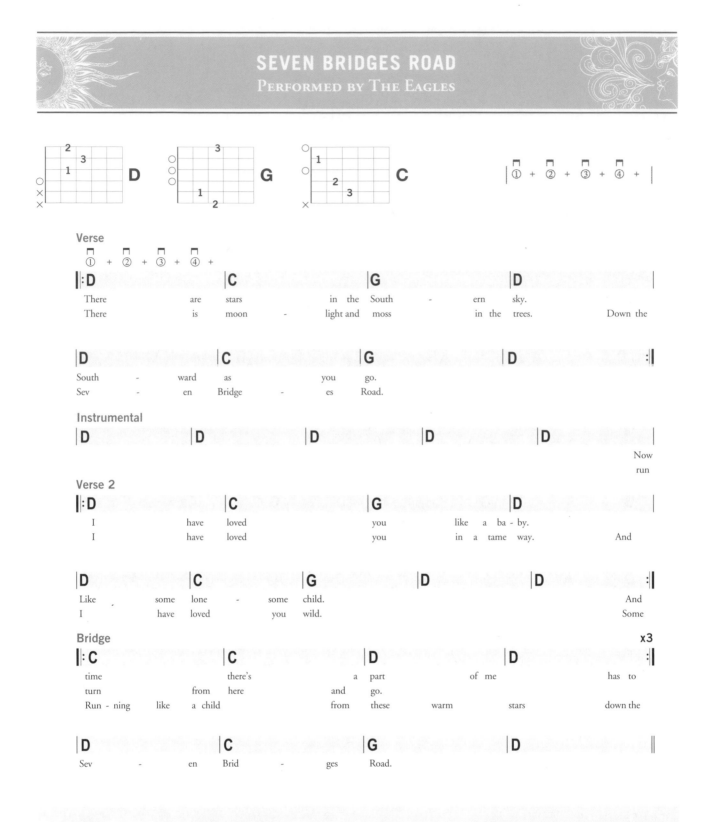

Verse

⊓		⊓		⊓		⊓	
①	+	②	+	③	+	④	+

‖: D | C | G | D |

There   are   stars   in the South -   ern sky.

There   is   moon - light and moss   in the trees.   Down the

D | C | G | D | :‖

South -   ward as   you go.

Sev -   en Bridge -   es Road.

Instrumental

D | D | D | D | D |

Now
run

Verse 2

‖: D | C | G | D |

I   have loved   you   like a ba - by.

I   have loved   you   in a tame way. And

D | C | G | D | D | :‖

Like   some lone - some child.   And

I   have loved   you wild.   Some

Bridge   **x3**

‖: C | C | D | D | :‖

time   there's   a part   of me   has to

turn   from here   and go.

Run - ning like a child   from these warm stars   down the

D | C | G | D | ‖

Sev -   en Brid -   ges Road.

VERSE 3
There are stars in the Southern sky
And if ever you decide
You should go
There is a taste of thyme-sweetened honey
Down the Seven Bridges Road

Seven Bridges Road | Words and Music by Stephen T. Young | Copyright © 1969 IRVING MUSIC, INC. | Copyright Renewed | All Rights Reserved Used by Permission

CLASS

THE GENTLE ART OF RIFFING PLUS A MINOR (THE SADDEST CHORD)

{ *How to count and play riffs; planting fingers to change between* G, C *and* D; A minor. }

ASTER THE GENTLE ART OF RIFFING THROUGH BASIC COUNTING

BLACK SABBATH! METALLICA! AC/DC! JOAN JETT! Besides a propensity for wearing black, these artists and many others share a tendency to not strum in a folksy manner. Instead, they "riff." A riff is a set of chords or notes played in a short and memorable pattern. Think of the introductions to **"Smoke on the Water" by Deep Purple** or the main guitar part to **"Seven Nation Army" by The White Stripes.**

There is no better first chord riff than the one used as the backbone for more songs than probably any other riff in existence. I am going to call it the **"Wild Thing"** riff, even though the exact same riff can be used to play **"Walking on Sunshine" by Katrina and the Waves,** the verse to **"All Star" by Smash Mouth** and hundreds or even thousands of other songs. We're going to learn this riff in the key of G, using open chords. (A "key" is a way in which skilled guitarists perceive order in music—you'll learn about keys in just a few lessons!)

First let's learn the G chord part. Count yourself in using eighth notes ("one and two and, etc.") and then boldly strum the G chord on "one" and "two." Remember that "⊓" means "strum down."

⊓   ⊓
① + ② + 3 + 4 +   1 + 2 + 3 + 4 +
|:**G**   **G** | :|

Now let's turn this into almost a riff. We're going to do something we've never done before: We're going to play a down strum OFF the beat on the "AND."

So now, very slowly, count and play the full first measure until you can do so in a reasonably confident manner four times through. Try to lead with your third finger when changing to the C chord.

⊓   ⊓   ⊓ ⊓
① + ② + 3 ⊕ ④ + 1 + 2 + 3 + 4 +
|:**G**   **G**   **C C** | :|

Next, learn the second measure of the riff. You'll strum with the exact same timing, only now going from D to C. Again, do this until you can play in a reasonably confident manner four times in a row. Try to lead with your third finger when changing to the C chord.

                              ⊓   ⊓   ⊓ ⊓
1 + 2 + 3 + 4 + ① + ② + 3 ⊕ ④ +
|: | **D**   **D**   **C C** :|

Notice that in both measures, the *C* chord is SYNCOPATED. In other words, instead of changing and playing ON the third beat, we play it OFF the third beat, or on the "and of three." This syncopation is the key to making **"Wild Thing"** and the various other songs built on this riff sound like they should.

Now, here comes the entire riff. Count and play slowly until you get the hang of this riff. Good finger plants will be extremely helpful when making these fast, syncopated changes. When changing to *G*, plant the second finger. When changing to *C*, plant the third finger. When changing to *D*, plant the first finger.

THE WILD RIFF!

Now, Learn this Chord to Make Your Listeners Weep with Raw, Ragged Emotion!

IT IS TIME for another emotional, poignant minor chord, the very famous *A minor* chord. In the movie *This Is Spinal Tap,* Nigel Tufnel proclaims that *D minor* is, in fact, the saddest chord. But many take issue with this analysis, considering *A minor* to be even sadder. Below is a diagram of the *A minor* chord, often written as "*Am*".

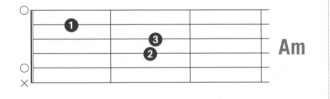

Am

I've heard people say that we think of major chords as "happy" and minor chords as "sad" simply through association—if you see enough movies of weeping people with a minor chord playing in the background, after a while a minor chord makes you want to cry, goes this argument. I think this is untrue—somehow the mathematics of the vibrations involved in a minor

chord just resonate in a particular way with humans. For example, I was listening to some classical music in a minor key with my 2-year-old son, and he said, "Dada, the violins are lonely." He knew, without being told.

The *A minor* chord is often used with the *C major* chord. What an easy change! You only have to move your third finger, and you strum five strings on each of the chords. Practice this change until you are reasonably comfortable and confident with it.

Your plant finger on the *A minor* is the second finger. In other words, when fingering this chord, begin with the second finger before adding the other two. Try changing between *Am* and *G* (six strings and also a second-finger plant) and then between *Am* and *D* (four strings and a first-finger plant) to get more comfortable with *A minor*.

```
⊓      ⊓      ⊓      ⊓        ⊓      ⊓      ⊓      ⊓
① + ② + ③ + ④ +    ① + ② + ③ + ④ +
|: G              | Am              :|
```

```
⊓      ⊓      ⊓      ⊓        ⊓      ⊓      ⊓      ⊓
① + ② + ③ + ④ +    ① + ② + ③ + ④ +
|: D              | Am              :|
```

A MINOR CATASTROPHE

SPEAKING OF *A minor*, I once taught one of the worst guitar lessons in my life with an *A minor*-laden song, "**Knockin' on Heaven's Door.**" Back before *New York City Guitar School* existed, I used to hold open "anti-procrastination" sessions in my apartment in Williamsburg, Brooklyn. I'd invite my illustrator/writer/thesis-writing/etc. friends over to drink coffee and work on whatever we'd been putting off. If I had a guitar lesson, I'd go into the other room to teach my student.

One day my friend Alia came over. Alia's cool—she hammers nails into her nose, eats glass, and lies on beds of nails as "Vulvina, Queen of Nails." But on this day she was just Alia, the professional illustrator badly in need of some concentrated drawing to meet an impending deadline. In she came, and she said, "Dan, how is it going?"

"Well," I said, "it's going great except that there's this song that's driving me nuts. It's 'Knockin' on Heaven's Door,' and I keep teaching it to people because it's the best song for learning *A minor*. But lately, every time I'm playing the song, I feel like darkness is closing in around me, and I feel like I've done nothing for my entire life except sing and play 'Knockin' on Heaven's Door,' and I think 'Is this it? Is this my life? Will this always be my life?' I've got to stop teaching that song, because if I do it one more time I'm going to jump out the window!"

> **Nigel Tufnel Proclaims that *D Minor* is, in Fact, the Saddest Chord. But Many Take Issue with this Analysis, Considering *A Minor* to be Even Sadder.**

Just then the doorbell rang. Alia retreated to the other room and began drawing furiously, and I went to the door. "Hi Lisa," I said, and in came Lisa, a gifted Broadway dancer and a brand-new-guitarist. We settled down with our guitars and she said "I'm so excited to learn 'Knockin' on Heaven's Door' today."

There was a single, loud and suddenly suppressed snort of laughter from the other room, and I began to laugh uncontrollably. In fact, I couldn't stand up!

"What's so funny?" Lisa asked. "Oh, nothing," I said, and we went on with the lesson, except that during each verse I'd start laughing again. Poor Lisa! Honesty is always the best policy, and I should have told her the full story. In retrospect she must have thought I was laughing at her, or perhaps that I was under the influence of some laugh-inducing substance! She never came back, even though she showed great promise as a guitarist. I remember that lesson with great shame as a teacher. On the other hand, ever since then I've loved to teach "Knockin' on Heaven's Door"!

The first time I heard "Knockin' on Heaven's Door," it was performed by Guns N' Roses. I liked it! A few months later I heard a very different version by Eric Clapton. I said, "Wow! Guns N' Roses are bigger than I thought—I can't believe that Eric Clapton covered one of their songs!" When I tried to impress an attractive girl with this piece of information, she informed me of what you already know: Bob Dylan wrote the song. Years later Avril Lavigne released her own version, and across America right now there are millions of people who think she wrote it! Sometimes I'll give a class a choice between learning an unnamed song by Clapton, Guns N' Roses, or Avril Lavigne. We'll discuss the pros and cons, and hopefully the discussion will become spirited. Then we take a vote, after which I reveal that we'll be learning a song made famous by all three artists.

Let's Review Some of the Fundamental Principles of Guitar Playing.

YOU ARE DOING QUITE WELL in your musical endeavor. You've learned to play chords and songs, and you are building the habits of a skilled guitar player. Most importantly, you recognize **that there is only one way to learn to play guitar—and that is to practice!** The more faithfully you pick up your guitar to play, the greater your enjoyment and mastery will be. In fact, practicing is itself a large part of the playing; the journey is the end.

When you form a chord with your fretting hand, you habitually **use your fingertips,** and you **finger close to the frets.** This allows you to expend the least amount of energy with the maximum results when fingering chords. Speaking of fretting-hand efficiency, you **leave fingers down when possible** while changing chords—this is called pivoting. Also, you **put the most important finger down first**—we call this finger the plant finger. With your strumming hand, you **consistently play the optimum number of strings;** your hand plays from the root note of any given chord.

You know that **music is made up of patterns.** You look for these patterns when you learn new songs, and doing so helps you to **learn songs by heart.**

Finally, you recognize that the key element of sounding great is to **play in rhythm.** Therefore, you tap your foot and you **lock your strumming hand in with the beat.** Furthermore, when changing chords you always **hit the new chord right on the beat.**

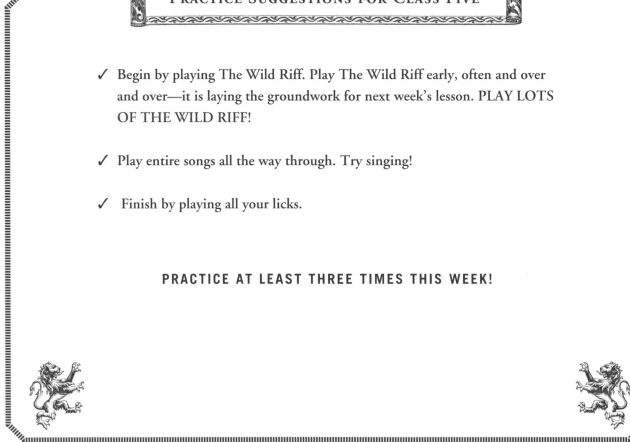

PRACTICE SUGGESTIONS FOR CLASS FIVE

✓ Begin by playing The Wild Riff. Play The Wild Riff early, often and over and over—it is laying the groundwork for next week's lesson. PLAY LOTS OF THE WILD RIFF!

✓ Play entire songs all the way through. Try singing!

✓ Finish by playing all your licks.

PRACTICE AT LEAST THREE TIMES THIS WEEK!

IF YOU WANT TO WRITE a hit rock song that makes people dance, I suggest you try working The Wild Riff into it. Very similar riffs drive songs such as **"Walking on Sunshine" by Katrina and The Waves** (capo III), the verse to **"All Star" by Smash Mouth** (very inconvenient with a capo, but very convenient in the future when you know barre chords!), **"Get Off Of My Cloud" by The Rolling Stones** (ditto), **"Hang on Sloopy" by The McCoys** (no capo needed!), **"Wild Thing" by The Troggs** (capo II) and others.

The Wild Riff

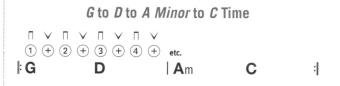

The following killer chord progression can be used to play **"What You Meant" by Franz Ferdinand** (open), **"Roses From My Friends" by Ben Harper** (open), and most notably for guitar players, **"Knockin' on Heaven's Door" by Bob Dylan** (open, covered famously by **Eric Clapton, Avril Lavigne,** and of course **Guns N' Roses**). Try playing with alternate strums.

Proto-Knocking

Of course, the *C major* chord is THE key chord of beginning guitar. By adding a *C* to the end of the *G-D-Am* progression, we get the essential harmony behind **"Closing Time" by Semisonic** (open), **"Hot N Cold" by Katy Perry** (open) and **"J For Jules" by 'Til Tuesday**

THE *A MINOR* CHORD
Learn the A minor chord to make your listeners weep with raw, jagged emotion.

(capo III). Oh, and just play the same repeating four chords only starting on the *Am* to get **"Who Will Save Your Soul" by Jewel** (open). Remember to leave your first and second finger down when changing from *Am* to *C*—just reach out with your third finger!

G to *D* to *A Minor* to *C* Time

As a guitar teacher, I love songs that follow common chord progressions, because it's so much easier to learn a song which repeats the same four measures over and over—and it is a nice bonus when those same chords in the same order can be used to play other songs.

But alas, sometimes songs are more complicated—like one of this lesson's featured songs, **"Impossible Germany" by Wilco**. When you play a song with such varied chord progression, try practicing each of the song's sections individually before playing the entire song.

Another of this lesson's songs, **"After Laughter" by Wendy Rene,** illustrates how music is shared across time and styles. The song was released in 1964 and despite featuring legendary organist Booker T. Jones, only achieved regional success. The song was famously sampled by Staten Island's very own Wu-Tang Clan in "Tearz" from their debut album *Enter The Wu-Tang Clan (36 Chambers)*. Since then, Wendy Rene's music has seen a resurgence, going on to be used or covered by the likes of Kendrick Lamar, Alicia Keys, and Ariana Grande.

Am is a great chord—but this chapter's most iconic milestone skill is changing directly from a *G* chord into a *C* chord. **"Mustang Sally" by Wilson Pickett** will help you master that skill. Begin with only one strum per measure and build up to the full strum pattern. Remember, it is perfectly OK to need hundreds or thousands of repetitions to get comfortable with changing directly to *C!*

IMPOSSIBLE GERMANY
PERFORMED BY WILCO

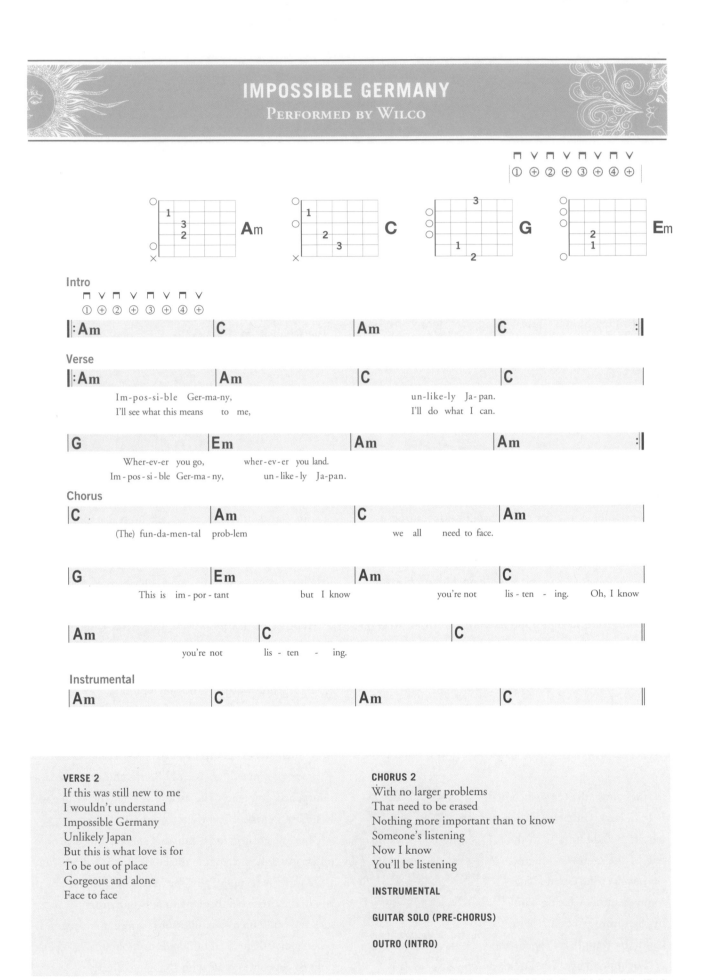

Intro

‖: Am | C | Am | C :‖

Verse

‖: Am | Am | C | C |

Im-pos-si-ble Ger-ma-ny,   un-like-ly Ja-pan.
I'll see what this means   to me,   I'll do what I can.

| G | Em | Am | Am :‖

Wher-ev-er you go,   wher-ev-er you land.
Im-pos-si-ble Ger-ma-ny,   un-like-ly Ja-pan.

Chorus

| C | Am | C | Am |

(The) fun-da-men-tal prob-lem   we all   need to face.

| G | Em | Am | C |

This is im-por-tant   but I know   you're not   lis-ten-ing.   Oh, I know

| Am | C | C ‖

you're not   lis-ten-ing.

Instrumental

| Am | C | Am | C ‖

VERSE 2
If this was still new to me
I wouldn't understand
Impossible Germany
Unlikely Japan
But this is what love is for
To be out of place
Gorgeous and alone
Face to face

CHORUS 2
With no larger problems
That need to be erased
Nothing more important than to know
Someone's listening
Now I know
You'll be listening

INSTRUMENTAL

GUITAR SOLO (PRE-CHORUS)

OUTRO (INTRO)

Impossible Germany | Words and Music by Jeff Tweedy, Mikael Jorgensen, Nels Cline, Glenn Kotche, John Chadwick Stirratt and Pat Sansone | Copyright © 2007 Words Ampersand Music, Jorgenstormusic, Nebsonic Music, Pear Blossom Music, Poeyfarre Music and These Four Songs | All Rights Administered by BMG Rights Management (US) LLC | All Rights Reserved Used by Permission

MUSTANG SALLY
PERFORMED BY WILSON PICKETT

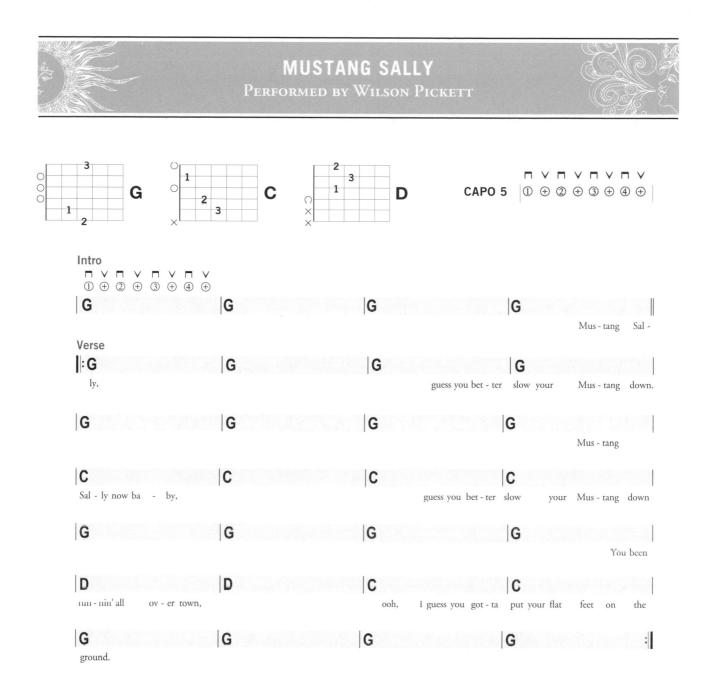

Intro

G	G	G	G ‖

Mus - tang Sal -

Verse

‖: G	G	G	G

ly,   guess you bet - ter slow your   Mus - tang down.

G	G	G	G

Mus - tang

C	C	C	C

Sal - ly now ba - by,   guess you bet - ter slow   your Mus - tang down

G	G	G	G

You been

D	D	C	C

run - nin' all   ov - er town,   ooh, I guess you got - ta put your flat feet on the

G	G	G	G :‖

ground.

CHORUS (VERSE)

All you want to do is ride around Sally
(Ride, Sally, ride)
All you want to do is ride around Sally
(Ride, Sally, ride)
All you want to do is ride around Sally
(Ride, Sally, ride)
One of these early mornings oh
You gonna be wiping your weeping eyes

VERSE 2

I bought you a brand new Mustang
A nineteen sixty-five
Now you come around signifying
   a woman
You don't wanna let me ride
Mustang Sally now baby
Guess you better slow that
   mustang down
You been runnin' all over the town
Oh! I'll have to put your flat feet
   on the ground
(What I said now)

CHORUS (VERSE)

All you want to do is ride around Sally
(Ride, Sally, ride)
All you want to do is ride around Sally
(Ride, Sally, ride)
All you want to do is ride around Sally
(Ride, Sally, ride)

AFTER LAUGHTER (COMES TEARS)
PERFORMED BY WENDY RENE

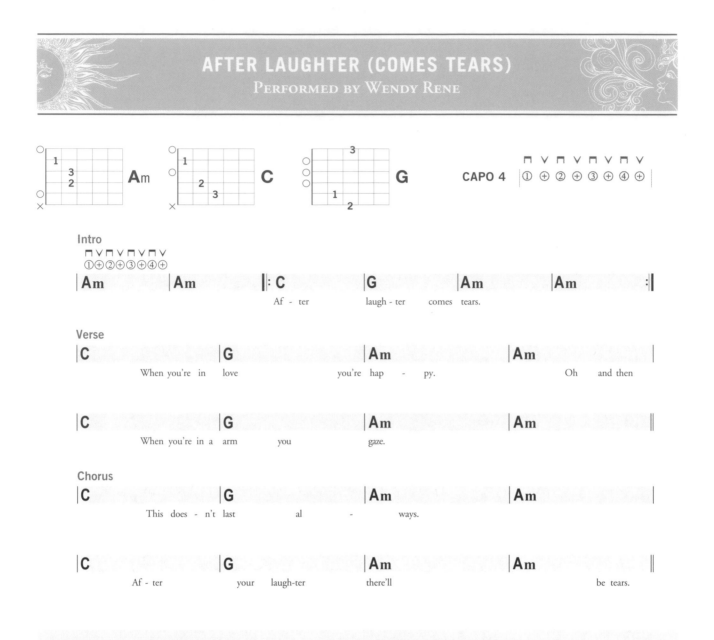

Intro

|Am |Am ‖: C |G |Am |Am :‖

Af - ter   laugh - ter   comes   tears.

Verse

|C |G |Am |Am |

When you're in   love   you're hap - py.   Oh   and then

|C |G |Am |Am ‖

When you're in a   arm   you   gaze.

Chorus

|C |G |Am |Am |

This does - n't last   al   -   ways.

|C |G |Am |Am ‖

Af - ter   your   laugh-ter   there'll   be   tears.

VERSE 2
My friends all say, "Don't try to hold it."
But I can't let that guy know how I feel

CHORUS
(After laughter comes tears)
I'll try to hold back my, my, my tears
But they keep say...
(After laughter comes tears)
After your laughter—oh! Oh! Ohhh

VERSE 3
I'll try to hide, hide my sorrows
I wonder, can I hold them till tomorrow

CHORUS
(After laughter comes tears)
Maybe, I'll hold them for a year
But they keep say...
(After laughter comes tears)
After your laughter,
   now you will see those wet little tears
(After laughter comes tears)
After your laughter,
   a little biddy tear will a-climb into your eye
(After laughter comes tears)
After your laughter—oh! Oh! Ohhh!
(After laughter comes tears)
After your laughter, my, my, my, my, my, my, my...

CLASS

RHYTHM 101:
LEARN THIS AND UNDERSTAND
HOW STRUMS WORK

{ *The powerful "Basic Strum" pattern* }

AVE YOU EVER PLAYED air guitar? Have you played **blazing air lead guitar,** your fingers undulating like over-caffeinated garter snakes? You weren't sitting down, and you were having a good time, right?

Despite my years of intensive study of the actual guitar and hundreds of hours spent on stage playing actual guitar songs in front of actual people, I must admit that my greatest exploits came with my trusty air guitar in hand. Why, I can't even count the times that I casually tossed off a Chuck Berry solo note for note on my air Telecaster, often while simultaneously eating deep-fried potato products.

I achieved my greatest air-guitar triumphs as a "student" at the University of Idaho. I lived there for several years in a dormitory called Upham Hall, which featured a large communal shower room with six high-powered nozzles. Early in the morning, this room was occupied by a rotating cast of surly, hung-over young men. I,

however, was not one of those worthy class bound students, because staying up all night playing guitar and juggling made me too sleepy to get up before noon.

Anyway, at two or three in my typical afternoon, I woke up and experienced a momentary pang of regret at having missed lunch. I generally decided to make the best of it. "I'll work on my air-guitar skills," I said to myself, heading off to the giant shower room.

Alone, I turned on all six showers full throttle and as hot as possible. The roar of the water cascading and echoing against the tiles sounded a lot like the open throated cries of forty thousand people screaming "EM-ER-Y, EM-ER-Y!" The rising steam quickly cut vision to just a few inches, much like six powerful fog machines. The large tiled floor provided me ample room to leap, slide and duck-walk, and the scarring jets of hot water aided me in concentrating fully on creating the ultimate air concert for my fans. Best of all, thanks to the University of Idaho's "physical plant" (whatever

---

The Secret

to Playing Great

Rhythm Guitar

is to

Move Your Hand

with the Beat.

Usually this means:
ON the beat, strum DOWN.
OFF the beat, strum UP.

that is) the hot water never ran out. Sometimes it would be five or six in the afternoon by the time I staggered out into the hallway, pink and wrinkled and barely in time to get ready for juggling club.

Yes, those were good times, and I'm sure you can relate. But my point is, if you want to play guitar like a superstar, then you'd better work on your air-guitar skills!

Do you remember the secret to playing great rhythm guitar? It's locking your hand in with the beat.

For example, if you were to play a *G* chord with the alternate strums, on the beat you would strum down, and off every beat (on the "and") you would strum up. Try it:

```
⊓   ∨   ⊓   ∨   ⊓   ∨   ⊓   ∨
①   ⊕   ②   ⊕   ③   ⊕   ④   ⊕
‖: G                            :‖
```

Wouldn't it feel great to strum complicated, tricky strum patterns which mixed down and up strums? You CAN strum those strums—but first you have to learn to lock your hand in with the beat so completely that it keeps moving exactly in rhythm regardless of the strum pattern that you are playing. In other words, you must learn to properly **air strum!**

Proper Air Strums

To PROPERLY AIR STRUM, move your hand up and down; down on the beat and up off the beat—without making a sound. Your hand will keep moving even if you are not actually hitting the strings of the guitar. This is vitally important! Make a *G* chord, count aloud and move your hand with the beat, but don't actually hit the strings of the guitar. To show this, I've written a measure complete with count and the strum direction. Move your hand with the beat:

```
⊓   ∨   ⊓   ∨   ⊓   ∨   ⊓   ∨
1   +   2   +   3   +   4   +
```

Now let's practice articulating selected strums. Count aloud, move your hand with the beat, but only strum the indicated beat. It is important to place your air strums exactly in rhythm. Your hand will move DOWN on every beat and UP on every "and" and it will actually strum the strings only on "two."

```
⊓   ∨   ⊓   ∨   ⊓   ∨   ⊓   ∨
1   +   ②   +   3   +   4   +
‖: G                            :‖
```

Now try a solitary off-beat, in this case the "and of two," which will be played with an up strum.

```
⊓   ∨   ⊓   ∨   ⊓   ∨   ⊓   ∨
1   +   2   ⊕   3   +   4   +
‖: G                            :‖
```

Play through this next measure several times. It's tricky! Keep your hand moving with the beat, and strum the indicated beats and off-beats. You know, if you were watching from a distance, each of these exercises would look exactly the same—the hand would just be moving steadily with the beat.

```
⊓   ∨   ⊓   ∨   ⊓   ∨   ⊓   ∨
①   +   2   ⊕   3   ⊕   4   +
‖: G                            :‖
```

The Basic Strum

NOW YOU'LL APPLY your new knowledge to an actual strum. I call it the Basic Strum, because it basically sounds great on just about any song. Keep your hand moving, even on the "and of one" and the "and of three" when you aren't actually strumming. Please try to make these air strums exactly with the count. You never need to speed your hand or slow your hand—everything will be where it is needed when it is needed. I've written in the pick direction only when you actually strum, because I know that you will remember to lift your hand up on the +'s.

```
⊓       ⊓   ∨   ⊓       ⊓   ∨
①   +   ②   ⊕   ③   +   ④   ⊕
‖: G                            :‖
```

Some people call it the "Down, Down-Up, Down, Down-Up" strum, because that is how you do it. Others call it "The Country Strum" because it is used in so many country and folk songs. Play it until you begin to feel comfortable with it, then try changing chords as you strum.*

CHANGING IN RHYTHM

SMOKING! Okay, now we're going to play this rhythm as we change chords—from an *Em* to a *G,* so that we have that nice first-finger pivot to help us out. Count yourself in, tap your foot, and play:

```
⊓    ⊓ ⋁ ⊓    ⊓ ⋁ ⊓    ⊓    ⊓ ⋁ ⊓    ⊓ ⋁
① + ② + ③ + ④ + ① + ② + ③ + ④ +
╟:Em                    | G                    :╢
```

*LEARN THIS STRUMMING PATTERN AT NYCGUITARSCHOOL.COM/BOOKS

After you've done that a few times in a row, try the Basic Strum with a plant change, *D* to *G*. Here I've written the rhythm out without the pick direction, because I know that on the beat your hand moves down, and off the beat your hand moves up! Play this change through until it feels moderately comfortable.

```
① + ② + ③ + ④ + ① + ② + ③ + ④ +
╟:D                    | G                    :╢
```

Often beginning guitarists will say, "Hey, if I'm right-handed, why am I using my left hand for these tricky chords? Shouldn't I be using my very coordinated right hand for that?"

Left-handers will ask the same question except reversed.

Now you know the answer—the fretting hand merely SETS UP the music—it is the strumming hand that EXPRESSES the music! Therefore your dominant hand is the one that strums.

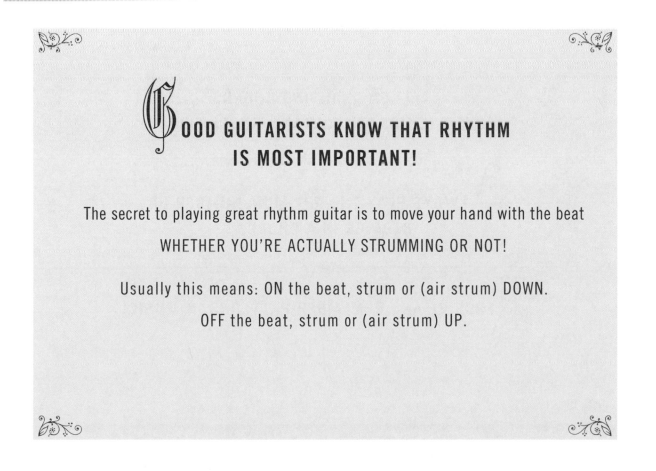

GOOD GUITARISTS KNOW THAT RHYTHM IS MOST IMPORTANT!

The secret to playing great rhythm guitar is to move your hand with the beat WHETHER YOU'RE ACTUALLY STRUMMING OR NOT!

Usually this means: ON the beat, strum or (air strum) DOWN.

OFF the beat, strum or (air strum) UP.

GOOD GUITARISTS KNOW THAT
PLAYING IN RHYTHM IS MOST IMPORTANT!
The secret to playing great rhythm guitar is to move your hand with the beat.
Usually this means: ON the beat, strum DOWN. OFF the beat, strum UP.

Good guitarists are efficient.
LEAVE FINGERS DOWN WHENEVER POSSIBLE
—PIVOT, PIVOT, PIVOT!

USE YOUR FINGERTIP TO FRET NOTES,
ALMOST BUT NOT QUITE ON THE FRET.

STRUM EFFICIENTLY, USING REST STROKES.

WHEN CHANGING CHORDS,
MOVE THE MOST IMPORTANT FINGER FIRST.

ALWAYS PLAY THE OPTIMUM NUMBER OF
STRINGS IN A CHORD.

PERCEIVE AND REMEMBER PATTERNS IN MUSIC!

PRACTICE SUGGESTIONS FOR CLASS SIX

First and Third Practice Sessions:

✓ Warm up by playing The Wild Riff incessantly to get used to the *G* to *C* change.

✓ Then play your Class Four songs incessantly to get used to changing chords as you continue strumming. Sing along!

✓ Review the Basic Strum, then play your Class Six songs.

✓ Finish with concentrated Wild Riff practice.

Second Practice Session:

✓ Warm up by strumming through your Class Three and Class Five songs.

✓ Practice your Cool Licks.

✓ Review the Basic Strum, then play your Class Three and Class Five songs again, only this time using the Basic Strum.

✓ Play your Class Six songs.

✓ Finish with concentrated Small Barre practice.

HERE'S A GREAT WARM-UP FOR YOU! The *G* to *C* change is THE defining change of beginning guitar. So why not incessantly practice that change? Once you're comfortable with that, you're over the hump and building some serious guitar momentum.

And guess what? Lots of songs can be played by alternating just those two chords, from **"Bells Ring" by Mazzy Star** (open), to **"Boss D.J." by Sublime** (open), to **"Wheat Kings" by The Tragically Hip** (open), to **"Every Morning" by Sugar Ray** (capo I), to **"Jambalaya"** by **Hank Williams** (open) and **"Give Peace A Chance" by John Lennon** (capo I).

You can simply listen to the above songs and then try to figure them out by ear. If you need extra help or want to be prepared for various idiosyncrasies, don't forget to check out **halleonard.com** for songbooks, including our own companion songbook *NYC Guitar School: Songs For Beginners* or search **sheetmusicdirect.com** for "nyc guitar school" or song titles. Start with one strum per chord, and then work up to the Basic Strum.

The Most Basic *G* to *C* Song Ever

For this lesson's songs, we offer you country, rock and rap! From David Bowie to Lizzo to Willie Nelson, everybody uses *C* chords. And the Basic Strum sounds great on almost any song.

If you take the intro for **David Bowie's "Rebel Rebel"** you'll end up playing the same progression for **"Wanna Be Startin' Something" by Michael Jackson**. You don't even need to change from capo 2 (but it is super fast). Then move your capo up to fret five, and use the same progression yet again to play along with **"Dreams" by Fleetwood Mac**, As usual, start out with whole notes, and then build up to the Basic Strum!

Don't get intimidated by the blazing fast banjo picking in the introduction to **Willie Nelson's "Bloody Mary Morning,"** the tempo of the song itself isn't as fast as it might seem. Just remember to bob your head, or tap your foot along with the recording to make sure you keep a nice steady and easy tempo! At the time of the publishing of this book **Lizzo's "Truth Hurts"** has gone septuple platinum. Originally released in 2017, the song achieved massive success on social media two years after the fact, and went on to win Lizzo the Best Pop Solo Performance at the 2020 Grammy Awards. The song does use some strong language which we've redacted so we can include it. So every time you see "***" in the lyrics, just sing "golly," "shucks" or your choice of choice words.

By the way, if you're an aspiring songwriter, try making up some lyrics as you repeatedly change between a *G* and a *C*. It worked for hundreds of other songwriters—why not you?

REBEL REBEL
PERFORMED BY DAVID BOWIE

CAPO 2

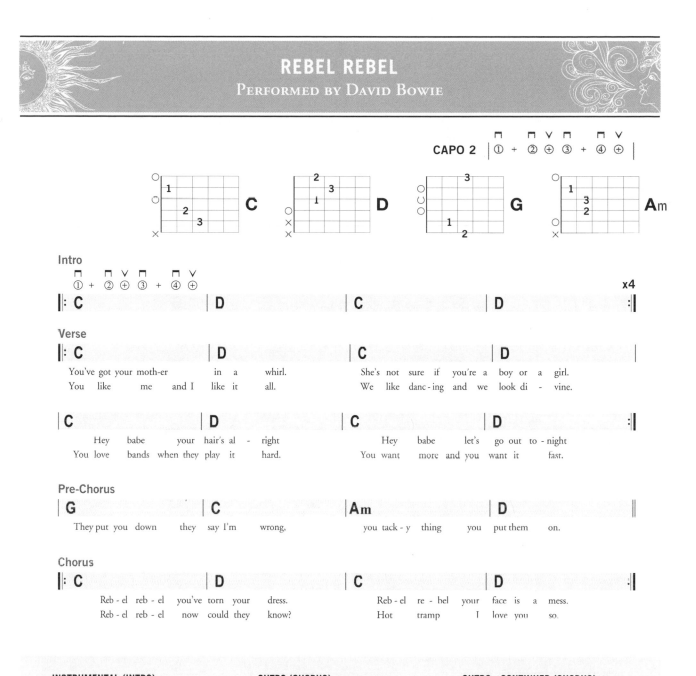

Intro x4

| C | D | C | D |

Verse

| C | D | C | D |

You've got your moth-er   in a   whirl.   She's not sure if you're a boy or a girl.
You   like   me   and I like it   all.   We   like danc-ing and we look di - vine.

| C | D | C | D |

Hey   babe   your hair's al - right   Hey   babe   let's   go out to - night
You love   bands when they play it   hard.   You   want   more and you want it   fast.

Pre-Chorus

| G | C | Am | D |

They put you down   they say I'm   wrong,   you tack - y thing   you put them   on.

Chorus

| C | D | C | D |

Reb - el reb - el you've torn your   dress.   Reb - el re - bel your face is a mess.
Reb - el reb - el   now could they   know?   Hot   tramp   I   love you   so.

INSTRUMENTAL (INTRO)

VERSE

PRE-CHORUS

CHORUS

INSTRUMENTAL (INTRO)

CHORUS

BRIDGE (INTRO)

OUTRO (CHORUS)

You've torn your dress,
    your face is a mess
You can't get enough,
    but enough ain't the test
You've got your transmission
    and your live wire
You got your cue line and
    a handful of ludes
You wanna be there when
    they count up the dudes
And I love your dress
You're a juvenile success
Because your face is a mess
So how could they know?
I said, how could they know?

OUTRO - CONTINUED (CHORUS)

So what you wanna know?
Calamity's child, chi-chi, chi-chi
Where'd you wanna go?
What can I do for you? Looks like I've
    been there too
'Cause you've torn your dress
And your face is a mess
Ooh, your face is a mess
Ooh, ooh, so how could they know?
Ah, ah, how could they know?
Ah, ah

BLOODY MARY MORNING
PERFORMED BY WILLIE NELSON

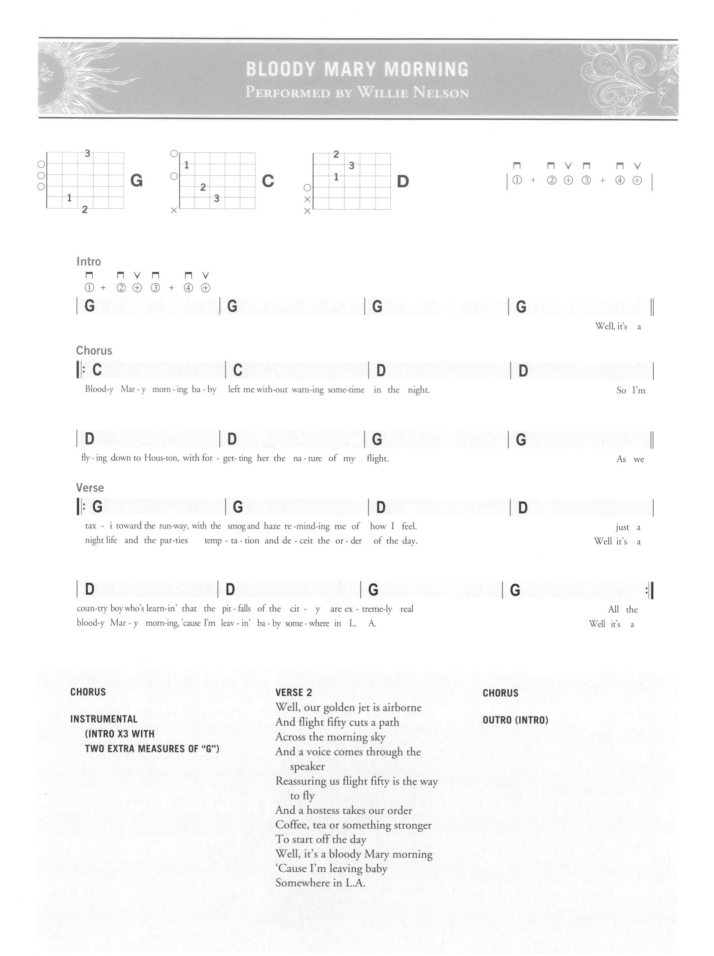

Intro

|G |G |G |G ||

Well, it's a

Chorus

|: C |C |D |D |

Blood-y Mar-y morn-ing ba-by left me with-out warn-ing some-time in the night.

So I'm

|D |D |G |G ||

fly-ing down to Hous-ton, with for-get-ting her the na-ture of my flight.

As we

Verse

|: G |G |D |D |

tax - i toward the run-way, with the smog and haze re-mind-ing me of how I feel.

just a

night life and the par-ties temp - ta-tion and de-ceit the or-der of the day.

Well it's a

|D |D |G |G   :|

coun-try boy who's learn-in' that the pit-falls of the cit - y are ex - treme-ly real

All the

blood-y Mar-y morn-ing, 'cause I'm leav-in' ba-by some-where in L. A.

Well it's a

CHORUS

INSTRUMENTAL
(INTRO X3 WITH
TWO EXTRA MEASURES OF "G")

VERSE 2
Well, our golden jet is airborne
And flight fifty cuts a path
Across the morning sky
And a voice comes through the
    speaker
Reassuring us flight fifty is the way
    to fly
And a hostess takes our order
Coffee, tea or something stronger
To start off the day
Well, it's a bloody Mary morning
'Cause I'm leaving baby
Somewhere in L.A.

CHORUS

OUTRO (INTRO)

TRUTH HURTS
PERFORMED BY LIZZO

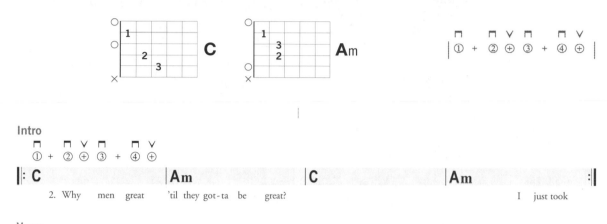

Intro

```
|: C        | Am       | C        | Am       :|
```
2. Why men great 'til they got-ta be great? I just took

Verse

```
|: C        | Am       | C        | Am       :|
```
D-N-A test, turns out I'm a hun-dred per - cent that ***** e - ven when I'm cry-in' cra - zy. Yeah, I
got boy prob-lems, that's the hu - man in me. Bling, bling then I solve 'em that's the god-dess in me. You could a had a
bad *****, non-com-mit-tal, help you with your ca - reer just a lit - tle. You're 'posed to hold me
down, but you're hold-in' me back. And that's the sound of me not call-ing you back.

Chorus

```
|: C        | Am       | C        | Am       :|
```
Why men great 'til they got-ta be great? Don't text me tell it straight to my face.
Best friend sat me down in the sa - lon chair. Sham poo press, get you out - ta my hair,
Fresh pho - tos with the bomb light - ing. New man on the Min - ne - so - ta Vi - kings.
Truth hurts, need-ed some-thing more ex - cit - ing. Bom, bom, bi, bom, bi bum, bum, bay.

VERSE 2

You tried to break my heart?
Oh, that breaks my heart
That you thought you ever had it
No, you ain't from the start
Hey, I'm glad you're back with your *****
I mean, who would wanna hide this?
I will never, ever, ever, ever, ever be your side chick
I put the sing in single
Ain't worried 'bout a ring on my finger
So you can tell your friend,
    "Shoot your shot" when you see him
It's okay, he already in my DMs

CHORUS

BRIDGE (VERSE)

I'ma hit you back in a minute (Yeah, yeah)
I don't play tag, *****, I been it (One time)
We don't **** with lies (Two times),
We don't do goodbyes (Woo)
We just keep it pushing like ay-ay-ay
I'ma hit you back in a minute (Yeah, yeah)
I don't play tag, *****, I been it (One time)
We don't **** with lies (Two times),
We don't do goodbyes (Woo)
We just keep it pushing like ay-ay-ay (Woo)

CHORUS

OUTRO (INTRO)

Many students continue their musical journey in our Rock Band program or in community jams around the city. (That's me in the NYCGS T-shirt at left, stepping thru beautiful guitarists in Union Square.)

CLASS

7

LEARN THE BEST STRUM AND ALWAYS SOUND TERRIFIC

— SPECIAL CLASS TEN NOTE! —

{ *Class Ten, which is your MASSIVE MOMENT OF GLORY, is coming up in just a few weeks. That's right—in Class Ten you will have the opportunity as a class to informally perform a song for an audience of several NYCGS staff and students as well as any friends or relatives you wish to invite.* }

 **:** *Who exactly is performing?*
A: Your entire class, including your teacher!

Q: *Should I feel nervous about this?*
A: Absolutely not. You'll have lots of company strumming, your audience will generally be fewer than five people, and they will be very friendly, too.

Q: *Why do we do this?*
A: At *New York City Guitar School*, we have found that students who play in front of others are massively more successful in playing guitar. Even just strumming a *D* chord in front of others forces you to achieve a higher level of mastery with the *D* chord and strumming. Playing in front of others is a breakthrough point as big as learning to change chords in rhythm!

Q: *Can I play a song by myself?*
A: Absolutely, if you would like to. Just let your teacher know!

Q: *How about with a friend or classmate?*
A: Absolutely!

Q: *What if I'm using this book on my own, and I'm not in classes at the school?*
A: Don't miss out on the chance to challenge yourself—and to celebrate your progress. Make a date with a friend! Or commit to recording and sharing a video! Or visit **NYCGuitarSchool.com/events** and sign up a virtual open mic night—we'll be excited to see and hear you. Oh—and it's never too late to officially join our school for virtual classes with other awesome students from around New York City—and the world!

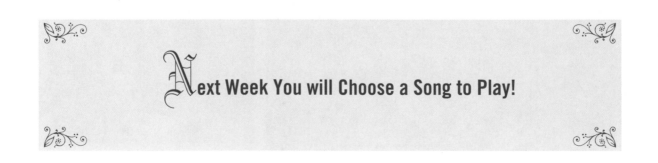

Next Week You will Choose a Song to Play!

The Basic Strum sounds great and is used in many, many songs. But there is one strumming pattern which is used even more. In fact, this strum sounds so good that many people learn it and never bother to learn any other strum. At *New York City Guitar School* we call it "the Best Strum." Master the material in this lesson, and you'll have a strum that will make you sound like a pro on virtually every song for the rest of your life!

Let's review alternate strumming. First and most importantly, remember that:

The secret to playing great rhythm guitar is to move your hand with the beat.

Usually this means: ON the beat, strum DOWN. OFF the beat, strum UP.

Review air strums. Make a *G* chord, count aloud and move your hand with the beat, but don't actually hit the strings of the guitar. Move your hand with the beat!

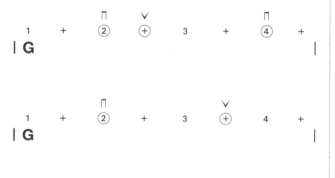

Review articulating a strum here or there. Count aloud, move your hand with the beat, and strum the indicated beats for the next several exercises. Place your air strums exactly in rhythm. Your hand will move **down** on every beat and **up** on every "and" and will actually strum only on the circled beats. **Keep your hand moving even when you are not strumming!**

And here are several reviews of THE BASIC STRUM. I've included some redundant rhythm notation to subliminally prepare you for future musical exploits. Don't be alarmed!

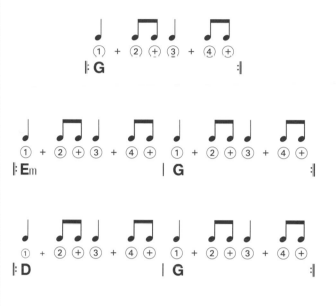

THE BEST STRUM*

BEGIN BUILDING UP to the full best-strum rhythm by air strumming your way into this bar. Repeat it a few times. **Keep your hand moving on the 1 + 2 + 3. Keep your hand moving with the beat whether or not you are actually strumming!**

Now leap into the Best Strum. Try it once through nice and slow. The key is: **move your hand down on the "three"** (even though you are not actually strumming!)

MOVE YOUR HANDS DOWN RIGHT HERE ON THE "THREE" SO THAT YOUR HAND WILL BE IN POSITION FOR THE UP STRUM.

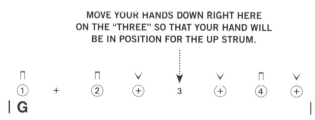

Then cycle through it. Some people call this the "Down, Down-Up, Up-Down-Up" strum, because that is how you do it. As long as your hand is moving with the beat, though, your hand will be moving in the right direction at the right time.

⊓   ⊓   ∨   ∨   ⊓   ∨
①   +   ②   ⊕   3   ⊕   ④   ⊕
| **G** |

Play it until you begin to feel moderately comfortable before progressing to chord changes.

BEST-STRUMMING WITH CHORD CHANGES

START WITH A PIVOT CHANGE—from an *Em* to a *G*. Tap your foot, count yourself in and play. You never need to speed your hand or slow your hand—everything will be where it is needed when it is needed. Remember to leave your first finger down on the fret while you change chords.

⊓   ⊓ ∨   ∨ ⊓ ∨   ⊓   ⊓ ∨   ∨ ⊓ ∨
① + ② ⊕ 3 ⊕ ④ ⊕   ① + ② ⊕ 3 ⊕ ④ ⊕
‖ **E**m | **G**   ‖

After you've done that a few times in a row, try the Best Strum with a plant change, *G* to *C*. Begin moving your fretting hand right after the "four" as you maintain your strum. It is the job of the chords to keep up with the strum because RHYTHM IS MOST IMPORTANT.

CHANGE CHORDS HERE
↓

⊓   ⊓ ∨   ∨ ⊓ ∨   ⊓   ⊓ ∨   ∨ ⊓ ∨
① + ② ⊕ 3 ⊕ ④ ⊕   ① + ② ⊕ 3 ⊕ ④ ⊕
‖ **G** | **C**   ‖

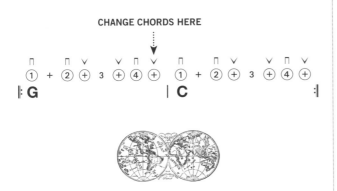

SOMETIMES IT'S JUST HARD

ISN'T IT TRUE that if you step back for a moment and take a clear-eyed look at where you are and where you've been, it is obvious that you have made massive progress in the art of guitar playing? Sometimes it is hard to maintain that perspective, though, when you're in the middle of trying to master yet another new and unusual guitar technique, rhythm or chord.

It's been about twenty years since I put away my riding-in-a-van-hustling-guitar-slinging ways aside. Since then I have devoted myself to making learning guitar as absolutely accessible, achievable and easy for my students as possible. "It's easy to play guitar!" I shouted. "Anybody can learn to do it!" I strove to make every chord, every progression and every piece of theory as easy as possible.

But one day one of my teenage students came in and taught me a valuable lesson. He said, "Hey, Dan—I just realized something."

"What?" I asked.

"Sometimes guitar playing is just not easy" he explained. "Sometimes it's just hard, and you just have to keep working at it until you get it, and it takes a lot of time and effort."

I felt like I'd been hit by a thunderbolt. He was absolutely right. And in my effort to make guitar accessible to people, I'd actually been doing them a disservice by intimating that it was always easy to play guitar. No wonder my students sometimes got discouraged when it wasn't!

For example, for most beginning guitar players, the *G* to *C* change is a giant and inconvenient pain in the phalanges. Theoretically, it is easy to get comfortable with the change—after all, you simply need to practice the change somewhere between 1,000 and 2,000 times. But, practically, practicing changing from *G* to *C* between 1,000 and 2,000 times takes a lot of, uh, practice. And sometimes that's not easy!

The good news is that YOU CAN DO IT! And when you get tired, when your fingertips are sore, when you lose your focus, give yourself a pat on the back! In life and guitar playing alike, persevering may not always be easy—but you'll be glad when you can say "it was worth it!"

This is an important week of practice! You are nearing the end of the course—this is a vital week for solidifying what you've learned so far, so that you can understand new concepts in the final lessons.

First and Third Sessions

✓ Warm up with all your licks. Take your time, have fun!

✓ Play The Wild Riff.

✓ Play your Class Seven songs incessantly!

✓ Finish up with one of your old songs.

Second Session

✓ Review the Best Strum and use it to play your Class Three and Class Five songs.

✓ Review the Basic Strum and use it to play your Class One and Class Four songs.

✓ Play your Class Seven songs.

Q: *Dan, is it wrong to practice more than three times a week?*
A: Are guitars sometimes called "axes" because they are used to cut down trees?

Since The *G-To-C* Change is so incredibly important in guitar, why don't you once again warm up with some of the same songs from last week—only this time, try playing the Best Strum? Again, songs built on good old *G-to-C* type progressions include **"Bells Ring" by Mazzy** Star (open), to **"Boss D.J." by Sublime** (open), **"Wheat Kings" by The Tragically Hip** (open), **"Every Morning" by Sugar Ray** (capo I) and lots more which you will probably discover for yourself. If you feel inspired, you can even try writing your own song using these chords.

The Best *G* to *C* Song Ever

‖: **G** | **C** :‖

But what if you're feeling intimidated by the Best Strum? Fear not! One of this lesson's songs is **"Chain of Fools" by Aretha Franklin**. It sounds terrific with the Best Strum, and the chord changes are relatively simple—as in, there aren't any! With only one chord, you won't need to worry about changing chords and you can fully concentrate on locking your hand in with the beat as you become the best at the Best Strum.

Once you've gained some confidence with **"Chain of Fools,"** mix it up with **Usher's "DJ's Got Us Fallin' In Love"** or **Taylor Swift's "mirrorball."** Both songs use a basic four-chord progression throughout and are perfect for leveling up from **"Chain of Fools."** Then, after you've mastered all three songs, you're ready to play along with the upbeat **"Born This Way" by Lady Gaga.**

Leveling up, one step at a time, is a great plan for guitar and for life. With all of these songs, remember that the first step to playing the song is to listen to the song! Next, play the song with just a single strum per chord as you get used to the structure.

And then? Best Strum!

By the way, I wouldn't be writing this if Covid hadn't temporarily shut down all our school locations and challenged me and the *NYC Guitar School* team to figure out different ways to teach guitar. While we were shutting down, Taylor Swift was learning that all of her 2020 shows for *Lover* were cancelled. That's when she wrote **"mirrorball."** The song's line *"They called off the circus, burned the disco down. When they sent home the horses and the rodeo clowns"* evokes that moment in time.

CHAIN OF FOOLS

PERFORMED BY ARETHA FRANKLIN

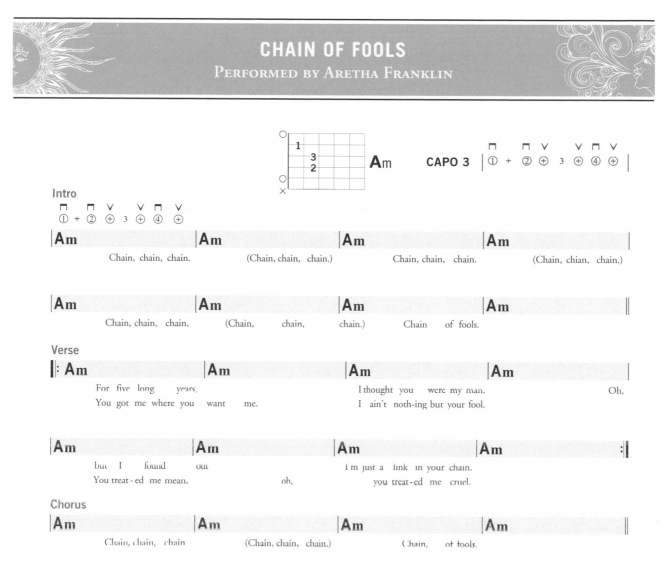

Intro

|Am |Am |Am |Am |

Chain, chain, chain. (Chain, chain, chain.) Chain, chain, chain. (Chain, chian, chain.)

|Am |Am |Am |Am ‖

Chain, chain, chain, (Chain, chain, chain.) Chain of fools.

Verse

‖: Am |Am |Am |Am |

For five long years, I thought you were my man. Oh,
You got me where you want me. I ain't noth-ing but your fool.

|Am |Am |Am |Am :‖

but I found out I'm just a link in your chain.
You treat-ed me mean, oh, you treat-ed me cruel.

Chorus

|Am |Am |Am |Am ‖

Chain, chain, chain (Chain, chain, chain.) Chain, of fools.

VERSE 2
Every chain
Has got a weak link
I might be weak, yeah
But I'll give you strength, oh, hey
You told me to leave you alone
My father said, "come on home"
My doctor said, "take it easy"
Oh, but your loving is much too strong

4. CHORUS 2
I'm added to your chain, chain, chain
(Chain, chain, chain)
Chain, chain, chain
(Chain, chain, chain)
Chain, chain, chain
(Chain, chain, chain)
Your chain of fools

VERSE 3
One of these mornings
The chain is gonna break
But up until the day
I'm gonna take all I can take, oh hey

CHORUS 3
Chain, chain, chain
(Chain, chain, chain)
Chain, chain, chain
(Chain, chain, chain)
Chain, chain, chain
(Chain, chain, chain)
Your chain of fools, oh

OUTRO (CHORUS)
Chain, chain, chain
(Chain, chain, chain) Oh
Chain, chain, chain
Your chain of fools, oh yeah

Chain Of Fools | Words and Music by Don Covay | © 1967 (Renewed) PRONTO MUSIC, INC., FOURTEENTH HOUR MUSIC, INC. and SPRING TIME MUSIC, INC. | All Rights Administered by PRONTO MUSIC, INC. | All Rights Reserved   Used by Permission

DJ GOT US FALLIN' IN LOVE
PERFORMED BY USHER

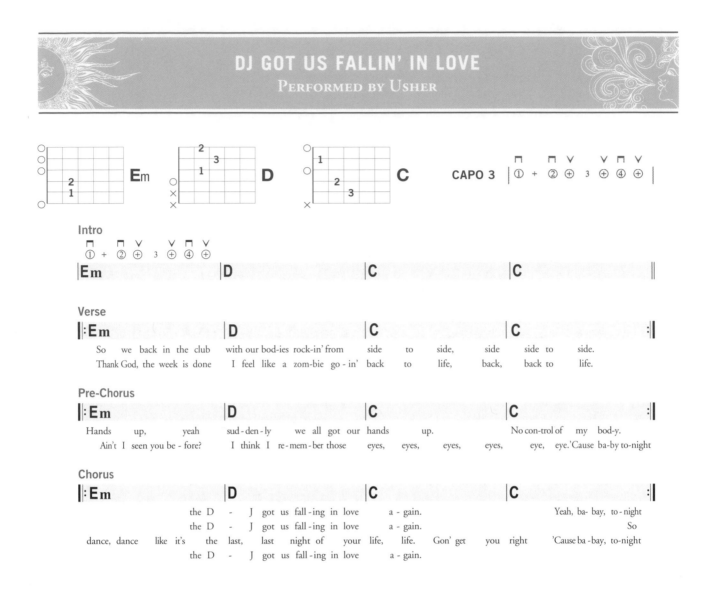

VERSE 2

Keep downin' drinks like there's
No tomorrow, there's just right
Now, now, now,
Now, now, now, now
Gon' set the roof on fire
Gonna burn this motherfucker
Down, down, down,
Down, down, down, down

PRE-CHORUS

Hands up
When the music drops, we both put our hands up
Put your hands on my body
Swear I've seen you before
I think I remember those
Eyes, eyes, eyes
Eyes, eye, eyes

CHORUS

BRIDGE (VERSE)

Hear no evil, I speak no evil, I see no evil
Get it, baby, Hope you catch that like T.O
That's how we roll
My life is a movie and you just TiVo, ha
Mami got me twisted like a dreadlock
She don't wrestle, but I got her in a headlock
Yabba-dabba-doo, make her bed rock
Mami on fire, pshh, red hot
Bada bing, bada boom
Mr. Worldwide as I step in the room
I'm a hustler, baby, but that you knew
And tonight it's just me and you, dale

CHORUS

BORN THIS WAY
PERFORMED BY LADY GAGA

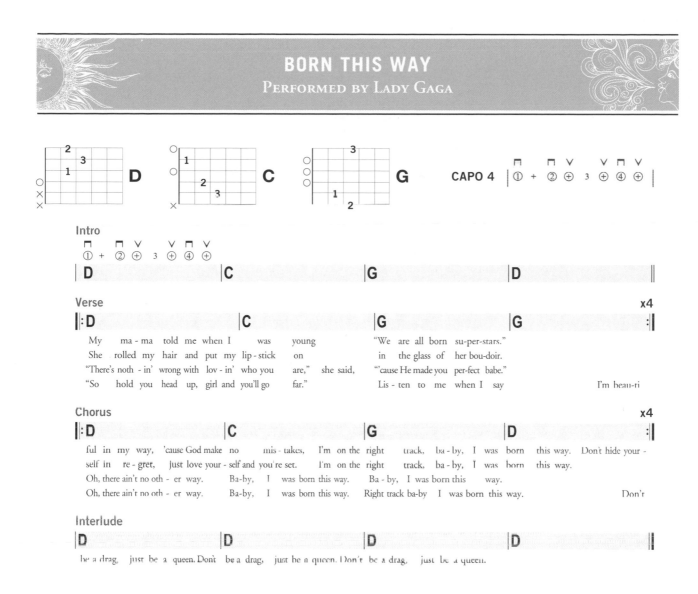

CAPO 4

Intro

|D |C |G |D ||

Verse

||: D |C |G |G :|| x4

My ma-ma told me when I was young "We are all born su-per-stars."
She rolled my hair and put my lip-stick on in the glass of her bou-doir.
"There's noth-in' wrong with lov-in' who you are," she said, "'cause He made you per-fect babe."
"So hold you head up, girl and you'll go far." Lis-ten to me when I say I'm beau-ti

Chorus

||: D |C |G |D :|| x4

ful in my way, 'cause God make no mis-takes, I'm on the right track, ba-by, I was born this way. Don't hide your-
self in re-gret, Just love your-self and you're set. I'm on the right track, ba-by, I was born this way.
Oh, there ain't no oth-er way. Ba-by, I was born this way. Ba-by, I was born this way.
Oh, there ain't no oth-er way. Ba-by, I was born this way. Right track ba-by I was born this way. Don't

Interlude

|D |D |D |D ||

be a drag, just be a queen. Don't be a drag, just be a queen. Don't be a drag, just be a queen.

VERSE 2

Give yourself prudence and
 love your friends
Subway kid, rejoice your truth
In the religion of the insecure
I must be myself, respect my youth
A different lover is not a sin
Believe capital H-I-M, hey, hey, hey
I love my life, I love this record and
Mi amore vole fe yah (Same DNA)

CHORUS

INTERLUDE
(Way) Don't be, don't be...
(Way) Church

BREAKDOWN (INTERLUDE)

Don't be a drag, just be a queen
Whether you're broke or evergreen
You're Black, white, beige,
 chola descent
You're Lebanese, you're Orient
Whether life's disabilities
Left you outcast, bullied, or teased
Rejoice and love yourself today
'Cause baby, you were born this way

BRIDGE (CHORUS)

No matter gay, straight, or bi
Lesbian, transgender life
I'm on the right track, baby
I was born to survive
No matter Black, white, or beige
Chola or Orient made
I'm on the right track, baby
I was born to be brave!

CHORUS

OUTRO (CHORUS)

I was born this way, hey
I was born this way, hey
I'm on the right track, baby
I was born this way, hey
I was born this way, hey
I was born this way, hey
I'm on the right track, baby
I was born this way, hey

Born This Way | Words and Music by Stefani Germanotta, Jeppe Laursen, Paul Blair and Fernando Garibay | Copyright © 2011 Sony Music Publishing (US) LLC, House Of Gaga Publishing Inc., Universal Music Corp., Warner-Tamerlane Publishing Corp. and Garibay Music Publishing | All Rights on behalf of Sony Music Publishing (US) LLC and House Of Gaga Publishing Inc. Administered by Sony Music Publishing (US) LLC, 424 Church Street, Suite 1200, Nashville, TN 37219 | All Rights on behalf of Garibay Music Publishing Administered by Warner-Tamerlane Publishing Corp. | International Copyright Secured All Rights Reserved

CLASS

How Great Guitarists Think About Music

{ *First, decide what song you will play in class 10!*
Then learn A *and* E *with pivots.* }

Before Learning How Great Guitar Players Understand Songs, Learn the Mighty *A* Chord

---

OOD GUITAR PLAYERS are efficient: They leave fingers down when possible. Make a *D* chord and the LEAVE YOUR FIRST FINGER DOWN while you make a new chord, the *A major* chord. Note that this is a five-string chord.

A MAJOR

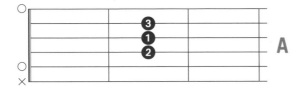

AH, THE *A major* CHORD. Mike Dulak taught it to me, back in Moscow, Idaho. Thanks, Mike, for teaching me my first guitar chord and banjo, too! (Mike didn't just play music—he built instruments and later founded the Big Muddy Mandolin company.)

You know *A7*. You know *A minor*. And now you know *A major,* which is usually just called "*A.*" You've got a lot of *A* chords! Did you know that there are many different ways to finger a chord? For example, many

good guitarists finger an *A* chord with their fingers in a row. Try it:

ALSO *A MAJOR*

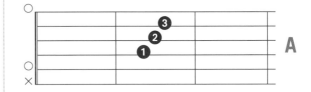

THIS IS A LEGITIMATE WAY to finger an *A* chord. But it doesn't give as many pivots or set up as many other future chord changes.

A year from now, you may use several different fingerings for each chord you know. Right now, give yourself a strong foundation for future guitar playing by using the first fingering given. Spend a few minutes changing between *D* and *A* leaving your first finger down, without counting. When you start to feel comfortable, add the Best Strum.

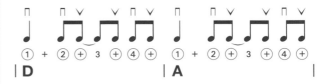

Continue Preparing to Understand Songs with the Mighty *E* Chord with a SLIDING Pivot

GOOD GUITAR PLAYERS are efficient: They leave fingers down when possible. Make a *D* chord and then **slide your first finger on the third string** while you make a new chord, the *E major* chord. Your fingertip will never leave the third string, even though you are changing frets.

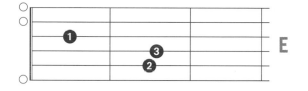

E

Now change between *D* and *E*. Begin with just one strum per measure, and work up to the Best Strum. **Keep your first finger down!**

```
  Π   Π  V     V  Π  V     Π      Π  V     V  Π  V
  ①  +  ②  +  3  +  ④  +   ①  +  ②  +  3  +  ④  +
: D                      | E                         :
```

When you are finished with that, try *A* to *E*. Begin with one strum per chord and work up to the Best Strum again. **Don't pick up your first finger—instead, slide it along the third string.**

```
  Π   Π  V     V  Π  V     Π      Π  V     V  Π  V
  ①  +  ②  +  3  +  ④  +   ①  +  ②  +  3  +  ④  +
: A                      | E                         :
```

This progression is used in lots of songs, including **"Sympathy For The Devil" by the Rolling Stones** and the end of almost every blues song. It is a great progression for trying out your pivot changes. **Leave the first finger down.** Try it out!

```
: E                | D                  |

| A                | E                  :
```

How Great Guitar Players Think about Music

MUSIC THEORY involves perceiving the patterns in music. You've already done this by noticing that chord progressions usually happen in sets of four or eight. Now you will learn to notice even deeper patterns.

Do you remember our "Wild Riff?" Let's play it a few times:

```
 ①  +  ②  + 3  +  ④  +   ①  +  ②  + 3  +  ④  +
: G  /      C /  | D  /      C /            :
```

Jimi Hendrix is one of the many great guitarists who played this riff. Incredibly, he did not think of it as "*G-G-C-C-D-D-C-C*." Instead, he thought of it as a set of **relationships** among chords, which in this particular instance used *G, C* and *D*. Whenever he felt

like it, he used completely different chords to play the song, and it still sounded right, because he kept the relationship the same. That's what good guitar players do: They see structure and **relationships** in songs where the inexperienced player may see only a set of random chords.

Go to the circus and you'll see lots of parents and kids. When you look at them, you'll immediately identify a set as "probably a mom, a big brother, a little sister" for example. Later you may learn that their names are Miriam, Elijah and Neoma, and that

THE *E MAJOR* CHORD
If you ever want to play Johnny Cash songs, you'd better get good at playing E.

THE *A MAJOR* CHORD
The preferred NYC Guitar School fingering for an A Major may look convoluted, but it makes changing to D and E a snap, because you can use your first finger as a pivot.

they are my family—but you don't need to know those specifics to understand the relationships involved. As a human you instinctively sense the connections between people. Now you will learn the relationships between chords.

Q: *Dan, this music-theory stuff sounds hard.*

A: And yet, what you will learn today is shockingly easy given its power and utility.

BEGIN LEARNING MUSIC THEORY IN A SHOCKINGLY EASY MANNER!

Step one: Can you count on your fingers, starting with your thumb? Try it. Feel free to use the handy guide below. Note that I have used Roman Numerals as well as Arabic Numerals:

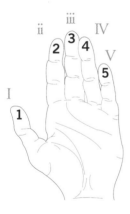

Step two: Can you say the musical alphabet? It is just like the regular alphabet, except that there are only seven letters: *A, B, C, D, E, F* and *G.* Whenever you get to "*G*" you start over with *A* again. The other wrinkle is that you can start on any letter. Study the following examples:

The musical alphabet starting with *A* is
A, B, C, D, E, F, G, A, B, C, D, E, F, etc.

The musical alphabet starting with *C* is
C, D, E, F, G, A, B, C, D, E, F, G, A, etc.

The musical alphabet starting with *G* is
G, A, B, C, D, E, F, G, A, B, C, D, E, etc.

CONTINUE LEARNING MUSIC THEORY IN A SHOCKINGLY EASY MANNER!

FOR REASONS having to do with the physics of music, any note is strongly related to the fourth and fifth notes following it. This is not a random relationship. These three notes, called the "first note," the "fourth note" and the "fifth note" are caused by vibrations which are mathematically related. They are **in harmony** with each other. In other words, they sound good! Practice counting on your hands as follows:

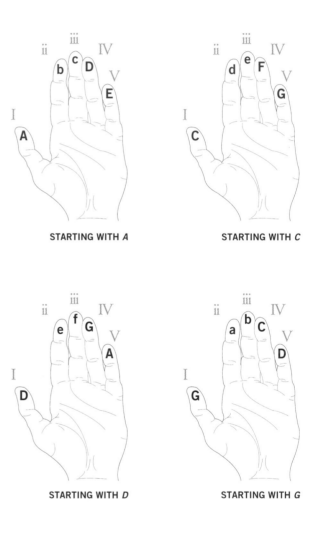

STARTING WITH *A*   **STARTING WITH *C***

STARTING WITH *D*   **STARTING WITH *G***

*In music theory notation, Roman numerals which represent major chords are typically written with capital letters, and Roman numerals which represent minor chords are typically written in lower case.

Songs usually start and end on the same chord. This chord can be called the "one" chord, and would be written as a Roman Numeral: I. The other major chords in the song are almost always the IV and the V chords. Because the I chord is so important, it is the **key** to understanding the song. When somebody says "étude in the key of *A major*" or "blues in the key of *A*" or "let's do this one in *A*" they usually mean that the I chord will be the *A*.

If we want to do a song in the key of *A*, what will the other chords be?

In the key of *A*, the I chord is *D*, and the V chord is *E*. In textbooks on music theory, this is usually shown with a chart. Fill in the rest of the chart. Feel free to count on your fingers or to refer to the hand diagrams. You probably don't know how to play all these chords. That's OK.

KEY	I Chord	IV Chord	V Chord
A	A	D	E
C	C		
D			
E			
G			

Let's return to Jimi Hendrix and The Wild Riff. Jimi could play it in the key of *G* just like us. Play it again.

$$ \text{①} + \text{②} + 3 \text{⊕} \text{④} + \quad \text{①} + \text{②} + 3 \text{⊕} \text{④} + $$
$$ \|: \mathbf{G} \quad / \quad \mathbf{C}/ \quad | \mathbf{D} \quad / \quad \mathbf{C}/ \quad :\| $$

But Jimi perceived the chord progression as a relationship which could be played based on any chord. He thought of it as:

$$ \text{①} + \text{②} + 3 \text{⊕} \text{④} + \quad \text{①} + \text{②} + 3 \text{⊕} \text{④} + $$
$$ \|: \mathbf{I} \quad / \quad \mathbf{IV}/ \quad | \mathbf{V} \quad / \quad \mathbf{IV}/ \quad :\| $$

Because he knew music theory, he then played that progression starting with any chord he wanted, for example, the *A* chord. So how does this song go in the key of *A*? Fill it in, referring to the Key of *A* chart as necessary.

KEY	I Chord	IV Chord	V Chord
A	A	D	E

$$ \text{①} + \text{②} + 3 \text{⊕} \text{④} + \quad \text{①} + \text{②} + 3 \text{⊕} \text{④} + $$
$$ \|: \mathbf{I} = \underline{} \quad \mathbf{IV} = \underline{} \quad | \mathbf{V} = \underline{} \quad \mathbf{IV} = \underline{} \quad :\| $$

Take your time. Refer to the charts, count on your fingers, and figure out how to transpose (that means "change") The Wild Riff from the key of *G* to the key of *A*. Play it a few times and notice that it definitely still sounds right; the chords are different but the song remains the same!

Q: *Dan, is this all there is to music theory?*
A: No. It just goes on and on and gets more and more complicated—but so what? I've heard that Mozart became frustrated because he couldn't understand everything in a music-theory textbook by the choral music composer Palestrina. Music theory is endless, just like quantum physics is endless. But you don't need to understand the theory of relativity to know that "what goes up must come down." And you don't need to know jazz chord substitutions or counterpoint harmony to know that *A, D*

and *E* sound good together! At this point we don't need to know about sharps or flats or relative minors or any of a million other things. The best thing you can do to prepare to learn these other concepts later is to pay attention to the I-IV-V theory that we learned today.

RETURN TO PIVOTS!

TRY OUT ONE MORE cool pivot with your new *A major* chord. This change is to *C,* and your second finger remains down. Start with single strums per measure and work up to the Best Strum!

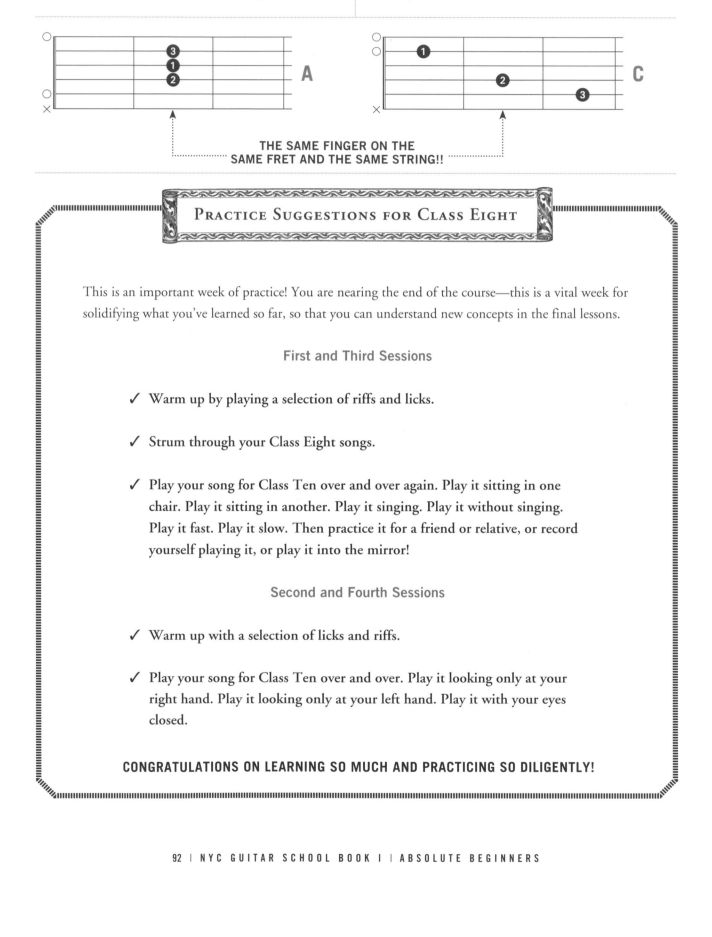

**THE SAME FINGER ON THE
SAME FRET AND THE SAME STRING!!**

PRACTICE SUGGESTIONS FOR CLASS EIGHT

This is an important week of practice! You are nearing the end of the course—this is a vital week for solidifying what you've learned so far, so that you can understand new concepts in the final lessons.

First and Third Sessions

✓ Warm up by playing a selection of riffs and licks.

✓ Strum through your Class Eight songs.

✓ Play your song for Class Ten over and over again. Play it sitting in one chair. Play it sitting in another. Play it singing. Play it without singing. Play it fast. Play it slow. Then practice it for a friend or relative, or record yourself playing it, or play it into the mirror!

Second and Fourth Sessions

✓ Warm up with a selection of licks and riffs.

✓ Play your song for Class Ten over and over. Play it looking only at your right hand. Play it looking only at your left hand. Play it with your eyes closed.

CONGRATULATIONS ON LEARNING SO MUCH AND PRACTICING SO DILIGENTLY!

IN THE KEY OF *A*, a I–IV progression would be *A* to *D*, which can be found in songs like **"All I Want Is You" by U2** (open) and **"In Between Days" by The Cure** (open) What? Just two chords? Yes—these great songs and many others are written off of just a couple of chords! After all, the essence of great guitar playing is not "lots of chords"—the essence of great guitar playing is LOTS OF EXPRESSION. Listen to **"All I Want Is You."** **The Edge** is playing his heart out with two chords—he's strumming them one way, then another. He's fingering them this way, then that way. He's adding a note. He's taking a note away. He can do this because his foundation is so secure—he's thinking of this song as a two-chord vamp and then he's letting his heart take over. Sure, you don't know everything that The Edge knows about guitar playing—but you know how it feels to be alive and to feel deeply . . . so warm up with these chords like you mean it!

All I Want is *A* to *D*

The **Lana Del Rey** song, **"Blue Jeans,"** will give you even more practice changing form *D* to *A*. Leave your first finger down!

Not the Blues

Finally, here's The Wild Riff again, only in the key of *A*, using *A*, *D*, and *E* instead of *G*, *C*, and *D*.

The Wild Riff

The next progression will allow you to play **"Pumped Up Kicks" by Foster The People.** Before playing along with the chart, take a moment to map out where your pivot fingers will be from chord to chord. Hmmm . . . *Em* to *G*, I can leave my first finger down. *D* to *A*, I can leave my first finger down. *A* back to *G*, I can leave my second finger down.

G to *D* will be your only change without a pivot finger! And that is no problem, because it is the first change you ever learned!

Pumped Up Progression

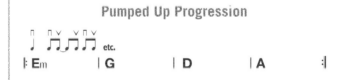

By the way, if you play the *Pumped Up Progression* and keep your capo on fret one, you can also strum along to **"Monster" by Imagine Dragons.** Put your capo on the third fret to tune in with **"Not Fair" by Lily Allen,** fret five for **"What Goes Around . . . Comes Around" by Justin Timberlake** . . . and if you slide your capo all the way up to the seventh fret you arrive at **"Radioactive"** —also by **Imagine Dragons.** (It turns out that not only do different artists use the same chord progression to write different songs, but sometimes the same artists use the same chord progression to write different songs.)

BLUE JEANS
PERFORMED BY LANA DEL REY

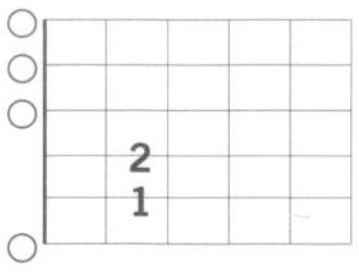

Em 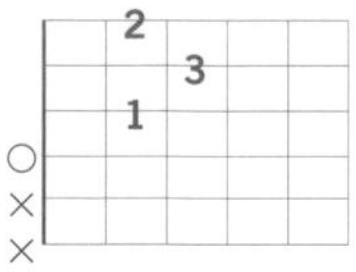   D 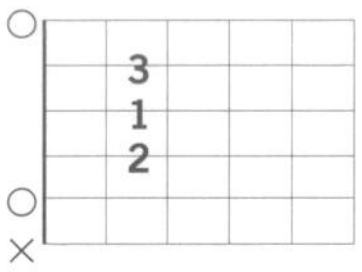   A   CAPO 1   ⊓ ⊓ V V ⊓ V | ① + ② ⊕ 3 ⊕ ④ ⊕ |

Verse 1

⊓ ⊓ V V ⊓ V
① + ② ⊕ 3 ⊕ ④ ⊕   x4

‖: Em | D | A | A :‖

Blue jeans, white shirt, walked in-to the room you know you made my eyes burn. It was
like, James Dean, for sure. You're so fresh to death and sick as ca - can - cer.
You were sor-ta punk rock, I grew up on hip hop, but you fit me bet-ter than my fav-our-ite sweet-er and I know
that love is mean, and love hurts. But I still re-mem-ber that day we met in De-cem-ber, oh ba-by!

% Chorus

‖: Em | D | A | A |

I will love you till the end of time. I would wait a mil-lion years.
Love you more than those * * * be-fore. Say you'll re-mem-ber say you'll re-mem-ber, oh ba-by,

To Coda

| Em | D | A | A :‖

Pro-mise you'll re-mem-ber that you're mine. Ba-by, can you see through the tears?
ooh. I will love you till the end of time.

D.S. al Coda
4x

‖: Em | D | A | A :‖

Big dreams, gang-sta, said you had to leave to start your life o-ver. I was
like, no please. stay here, we don't need no mon-ey we can make it all work. But he
head-ed out on Sund-day, said he'd come home Mon-day. I stayed up wait-in', an-ti-ci-pat-in' and pac-in' but he was
chas-in' pa-per. Caught up in the game that was the last I heard.

⊕ Bridge

‖: Em | Em | Em | Em |

You went out ev-'ry night, and ba-by that's al-right. I told you that no mat-ter what you did I'd be by your side.
a piece of me died. Told you I wan-ted more, it's not what I had in mind. Just want it like be-fore.

| D | D | D | D :‖

'Cause I'm-ma ride or die wheth-er you fail or fly. Well, shit at least you tried, but when you walked out that door.
We were danc-in' all night. Then they took you a-way, stole you out of my life. You just need to re-mem-ber.

CHORUS

PUMPED UP KICKS
PERFORMED BY FOSTER THE PEOPLE

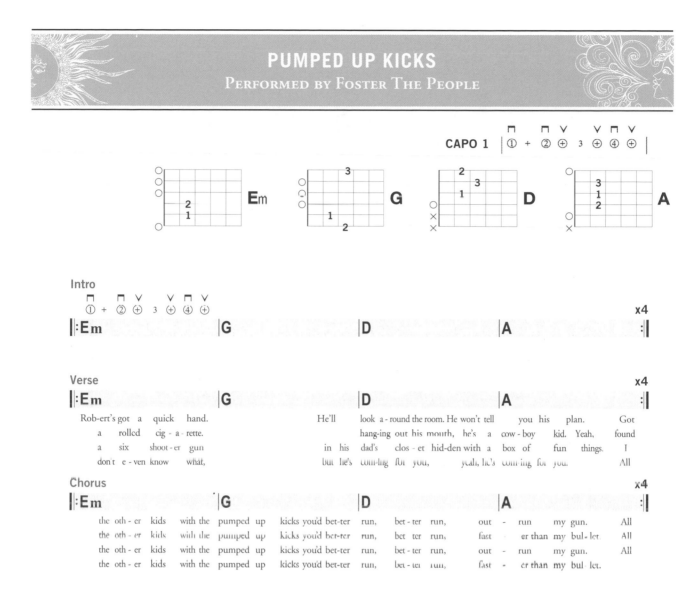

CAPO 1

Em   G   D   A

Intro

‖: Em | G | D | A :‖ x4

Verse

‖: Em | G | D | A :‖ x4

Rob-ert's got a quick hand. He'll look a-round the room. He won't tell you his plan. Got
a rolled cig-a-rette. hang-ing out his mouth, he's a cow-boy kid. Yeah, found
a six shoot-er gun in his dad's clos-et hid-den with a box of fun things. I
don't e-ven know what, but he's com-ing for you, yeah, he's com-ing for you. All

Chorus

‖: Em | G | D | A :‖ x4

the oth-er kids with the pumped up kicks you'd bet-ter run, bet-ter run, out - run my gun. All
the oth-er kids with the pumped up kicks you'd bet-ter run, bet-ter run, fast er than my bul-let. All
the oth-er kids with the pumped up kicks you'd bet-ter run, bet-ter run, out - run my gun. All
the oth-er kids with the pumped up kicks you'd bet-ter run, bet-ter run, fast - er than my bul-let.

VERSE 2
Daddy works a long day
He be coming home late, and he's coming home late
And he's bringing me a surprise
'Cause dinner's in the kitchen and it's packed in ice
I've waited for a long time
Yeah, the sleight of my hand is now a quick-pull trigger
I reason with my cigarette
And say, "Your hair's on fire, you must have lost your wits,"
   yeah

CHORUS

BRIDGE (INTRO)

CHORUS

OUTRO (CHORUS)

CLASS

RHYTHM 102:
MIXED RHYTHMS AND SPLIT MEASURES

— CLASS TEN NOTE —

If you're inviting guests to hear you play at your New York City Guitar School performance, ask them to come for the last 15-20 minutes of class. Are you studying on your own? Make an appointment with friends or family to play a song for them, sign up for a virtual Open Mic at NYCGuitarSchool.com/events, or plan to record a video to share on social media (tag @nycguitarschool).

IXED RHYTHMS

THIS LESSON continues to build on your fundamental habit of locking your hand in with the beat, even if you are not actually strumming. Let's play through each of our massively useful rhythms for a moment in order to prepare for mixed rhythms. First, the Basic Strum:

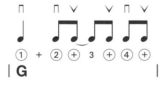

After you've played through the Basic Strum a few times, review the Best Strum:

Now you are ready to mix these two rhythms together. On the first measure you will play the Best Strum, smoothly continuing with the Basic Strum on the second measure. Remember to **keep your hand moving!** You will be playing a different strum pattern on each measure. Play the following line until you are moderately comfortable and confident with it. The chord remains the same—only the strum is changed!

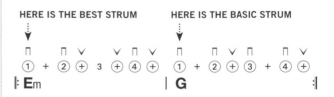

In a way, this will be easier with a chord change, because it will be easier to hear the two different patterns. Try a pivot change for a few times:

And now play mixed rhythms with a plant change, *D* to *G*. Here I've written the rhythm in notation and without the pick direction, because you remember that on the beat, your hand moves down, and off the beat your hand moves up! (In this class you don't have to read standard rhythm notation—I just put it in now and then so it will soak into you by osmosis and help prepare you for the next course.) Play through this change a bunch of times until you feel comfortable smoothly repeating the line:

$$\text{:} D \qquad | G \qquad \text{:}$$

Your Sure-Fire Method to Sound Great on Just about Any Song

As you know, some measures of music contain two chords. That means that you will often need to change chords in the middle of a measure. We can call these measures **split measures** because they are split into two chords. Here is a typical progression with a split measure:

$$\text{:} D \qquad G \qquad | A7 \qquad \text{:}$$

How do you strum this progression? Well, as a guitarist with ever-greater understanding and skill, you will soon discover that the possibilities are infinite. In the meantime, 99 percent of the time your songs will sound great if you play them with the Best Strum, except for split measures, which you'll handle with the Basic Strum. In fact, let's make a note of this:

Let's give it a shot. The following two-measure progression can be used to play **"La Bamba" by Ritchie Valens, "Twist and Shout" by The Beatles** and lots of other songs. Play through the example until you get modestly comfortable. The *D* will fall right on the "one" and the *G* will fall right on the "three".

HERE IS THE BASIC STRUM   **HERE IS THE BEST STRUM**

$$\text{:} D \qquad G \qquad | A7 \qquad \text{:}$$

The key, as always, is to **keep your hand moving.** Here's another typical two-measure progression to get comfortable with. It is the chorus for such songs as **"Imagine" by John Lennon, "Redemption Song" by Bob Marley** and numerous other tunes. I put it down in rhythm notation.

HERE IS THE BEST STRUM   **HERE IS THE BASIC STRUM**

$$\text{:} G \qquad | C \qquad D \qquad \text{:}$$

Good guitarists don't just bash away at the guitar with a single uniform strum all the way through a song. They are expressive and flexible. You will be too. Remember this:

A great default arrangement for virtually any song is to play all one-chord measures with the Best Strum, and to play all split measures with the Basic Strum.

First Session

✓ Play through your Class Ten song.

✓ Play lots of other songs.

✓ Play your Class Nine songs.

Second Session

✓ Warm up by playing your small barre licks and The Wild Riff.

✓ Play the progressions below incessantly:

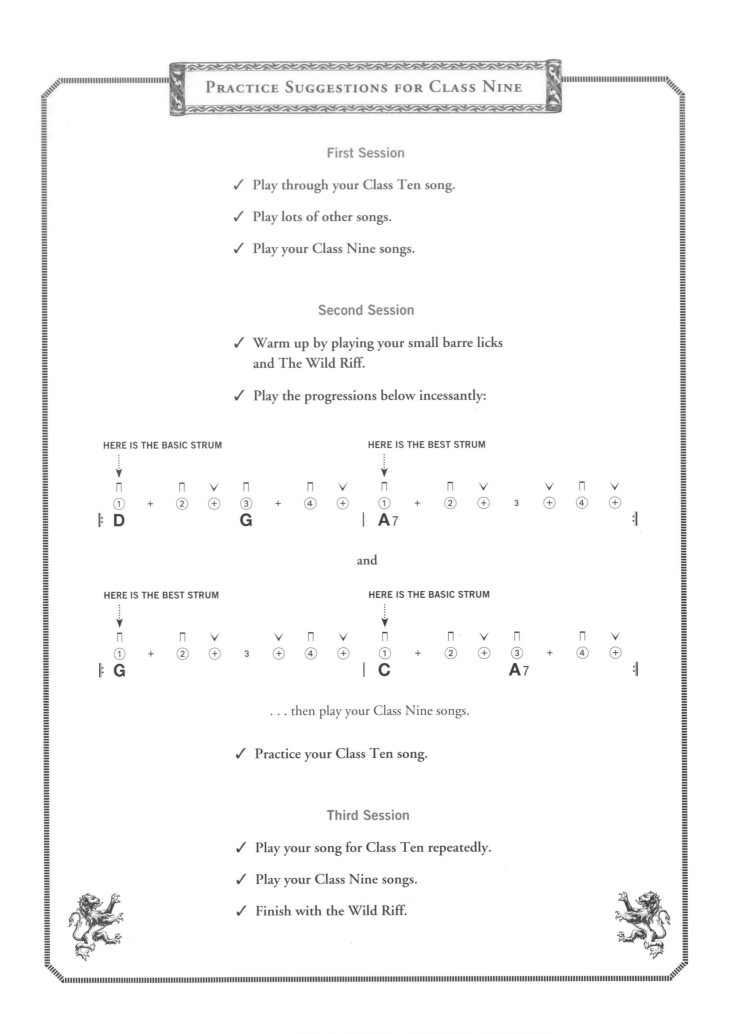

and

. . . then play your Class Nine songs.

✓ Practice your Class Ten song.

Third Session

✓ Play your song for Class Ten repeatedly.

✓ Play your Class Nine songs.

✓ Finish with the Wild Riff.

CONGRATULATIONS! You now have the chords and strums to have fun and sound good on a large proportion of rock, pop, folk, country, you-name-it guitar songs. As you put together your one-chord-per-measure Best Strum with your split-measure variant on the Basic Strum, there will be no stopping you!

Incredible quantities of songs are built off of a two-bar pattern like the one below, with the first measure split between *G* and *C* followed by a full measure of *D,* including "**Twist and Shout**" by **The Isley Brothers** (capo X) (**The Beatles** cover is more well known), "**La Bamba**" by **Ritchie Valens** (capo V), "**Make Me Lose Control**" by **Eric Carmen** and "**Stand**" by **R.E.M** both (capo IX).

```
⊓   ⊓ ∨ ⊓   ⊓ ∨   ⊓    ⊓ ∨   ∨ ⊓ ∨
① + ② + ③ + ④ +   ① + ② + 3 + ④ +
‖:G        C      | D              :‖
```

Play the same chords in the same order, but with a full measure of *G* and a split measure of *C* and *D* and you have the harmony behind "**Come On, Let's Go**" (also by **Ritchie Valens** [capo II]) and the choruses to "**Redemption Song**" by Bob Marley (open).

```
⊓   ⊓ ∨   ∨ ⊓ ∨   ⊓    ⊓ ∨ ⊓   ⊓ ∨
① + ② + 3 + ④ +   ① + ② + ③ + ④ +
‖:G            |C        D       :‖
```

As you'll see when you get to the chart, there's a lot more to "**Redemption Song**" than those two bars. It's one of your first songs to feature not only different verse and chorus progressions, but some variations even within those patterns. And of course there's that iconic opening part—if you're feeling ambitious and want to play some single notes, look it up!

"**Never Be the Same**" by **Camila Cabello** is another of this lesson's songs with a more complicated verse and chorus structure. It's also the perfect song for building confidence with your mixed rhythms, because each chord in the song gets two full measures—the first with the Best Strum and the second with the Basic Strum. Get comfortable doing that with just *G* before moving on to the rest of the song:

Never Be the Same Strum Pattern

```
⊓   ⊓ ∨   ∨ ⊓ ∨   ⊓    ⊓ ∨ ⊓   ⊓ ∨
① + ② + 3 + ④ +   ① + ② + ③ + ④ +
‖:G            | G             :‖
```

Watch out for the mixed rhythms AND split measures in "**Gold On the Ceiling**" by **The Black Keys**. And remember that your first finger never needs to leave the guitar as you pivot between *A, D* and *E.* These two bars may be the trickiest part:

First Finger On the Third String

```
⊓   ⊓ ∨ ⊓   ⊓ ∨   ⊓    ⊓ ∨   ∨ ⊓ ∨
① + ② + ③ + ④ +   ① + ② + 3 + ④ +
‖:D        A      | E             :‖
```

REDEMPTION SONG
PERFORMED BY BOB MARLEY

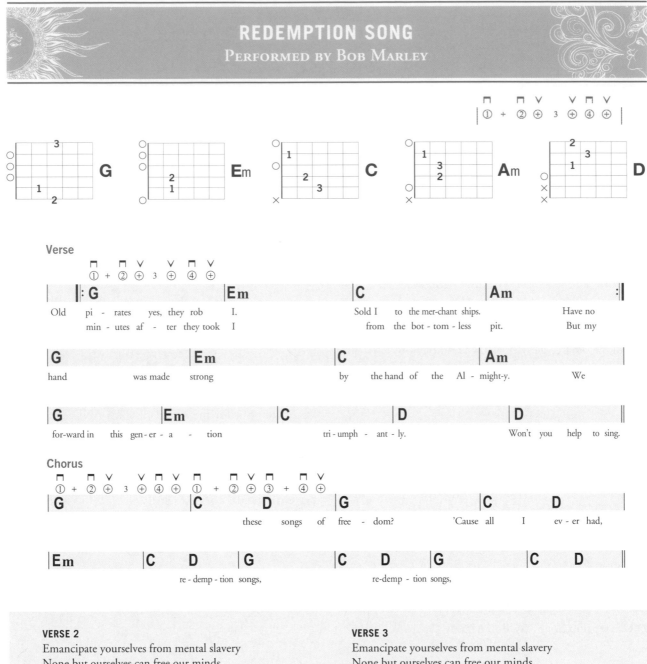

Verse

G	Em	C	Am :|
Old pi - rates yes, they rob I.		Sold I to the mer-chant ships.	Have no
min - utes af - ter they took I		from the bot - tom - less pit.	But my

G	Em	C	Am
hand was made strong		by the hand of the Al - might-y.	We

G	Em	C	D	D
for-ward in this gen-er-a - tion		tri - umph - ant - ly.	Won't you help to sing.	

Chorus

G	C	D	G	C	D
	these songs of free - dom?		'Cause all I ev - er had,		

Em	C	D	G	C	D	G	C	D
re - demp - tion songs,				re-demp - tion songs,				

VERSE 2
Emancipate yourselves from mental slavery
None but ourselves can free our minds
Have no fear for atomic energy
'Cause none of them can stop the time
How long shall they kill our prophets
While we stand aside and look?
Ooh, some say it's just a part of it
We've got to fulfill the book

CHORUS

ACOUSTIC BREAK

||: Em | C D :|| x4

VERSE 3
Emancipate yourselves from mental slavery
None but ourselves can free our minds
Whoa! Have no fear for atomic energy
'Cause none of them-ah can-ah stop-ah the time
How long shall they kill our prophets
While we stand aside and look?
Yes, some say it's just a part of it
We've got to fulfill the book

CHORUS

NEVER BE THE SAME
PERFORMED BY CAMILA CABELLO

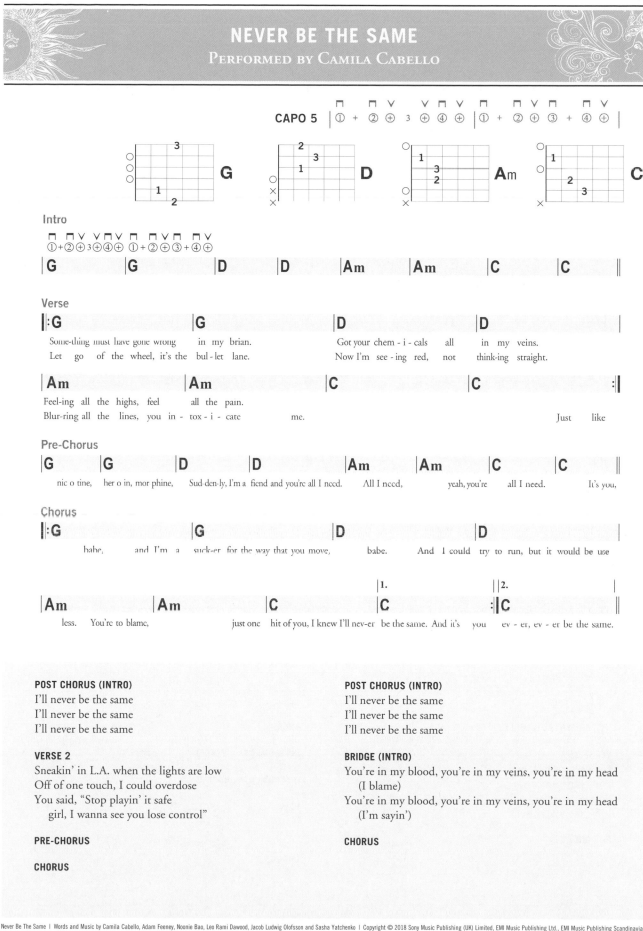

POST CHORUS (INTRO)
I'll never be the same
I'll never be the same
I'll never be the same

VERSE 2
Sneakin' in L.A. when the lights are low
Off of one touch, I could overdose
You said, "Stop playin' it safe
   girl, I wanna see you lose control"

PRE-CHORUS

CHORUS

POST CHORUS (INTRO)
I'll never be the same
I'll never be the same
I'll never be the same

BRIDGE (INTRO)
You're in my blood, you're in my veins, you're in my head
   (I blame)
You're in my blood, you're in my veins, you're in my head
   (I'm sayin')

CHORUS

GOLD ON THE CEILING
Performed by The Black Keys

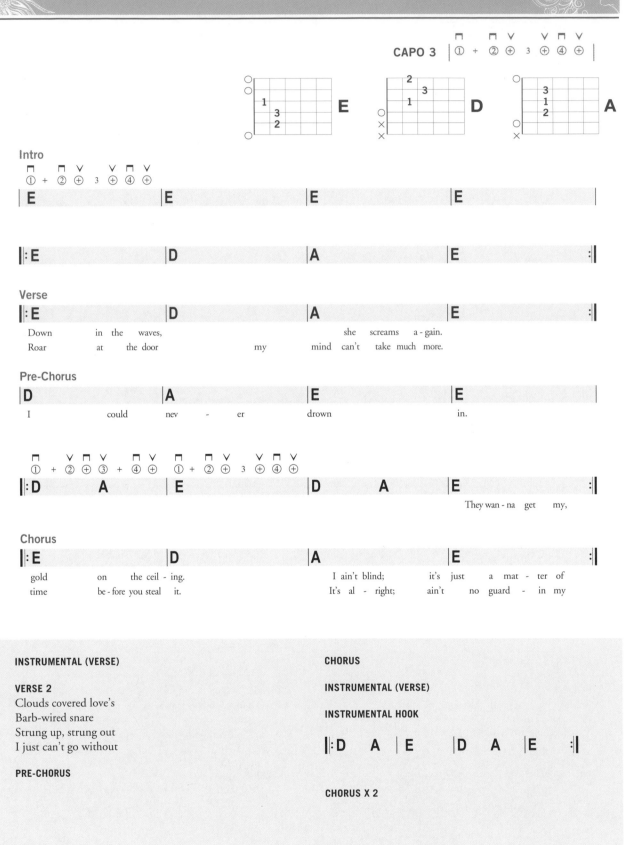

CAPO 3

Intro

E | E | E | E |

‖: E | D | A | E :‖

Verse

‖: E | D | A | E :‖

Down in the waves, she screams a-gain.
Roar at the door my mind can't take much more.

Pre-Chorus

D | A | E | E |

I could nev - er drown in.

‖: D A | E | D A | E :‖

They wan - na get my,

Chorus

‖: E | D | A | E :‖

gold on the ceil - ing. I ain't blind; it's just a mat - ter of
time be - fore you steal it. It's al - right; ain't no guard - in my

INSTRUMENTAL (VERSE)

VERSE 2
Clouds covered love's
Barb-wired snare
Strung up, strung out
I just can't go without

PRE-CHORUS

CHORUS

INSTRUMENTAL (VERSE)

INSTRUMENTAL HOOK

‖: D A | E | D A | E :‖

CHORUS X 2

CLASS

10

REVIEW, OPEN CLASS, AND GRAND FINALE!

{ *C O N G R A T U L A T I O N S !!* }

ONGRATULATIONS. If you practiced several times a week over the past two and a half months then you are a significantly improved guitar player. You know the most commonly used chords in guitar, you can strum on and off the beat, you can read chord diagrams and tablature, you can play songs, licks and riffs, you can play several of the most important strum patterns in guitar...you have made a tremendous amount of progress, and you deserve to be proud.

I'm writing these words in a book store near Madison Square Garden...my table is littered with empty coffee cups, and I've just finished proofing the final layout of this guitar manual, so I'm feeling a sense of accomplishment, too.

I'm pondering the effect of little steps over time. A finished book begins with a few words, and over time, repeated sessions of writing result in what to me is a bit of a miracle—a finished book! And every capable and confident guitar player began as a novice guitar player who knew nothing, but kept playing. Like you. Good job!

At your teacher's discretion you may just go right on to get some last minute practice in on your Class Ten performance song. Otherwise, let's review your massive array of new-found guitar skills.

CONGRATULATIONS!
YOU KNOW THE MOST ESSENTIAL GUITAR CHORDS.

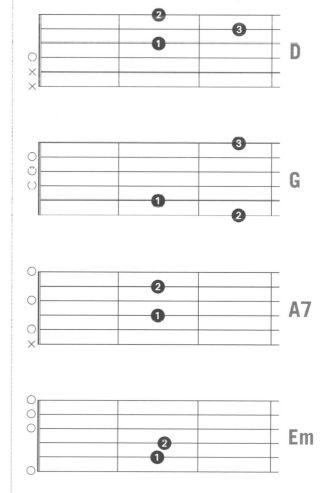

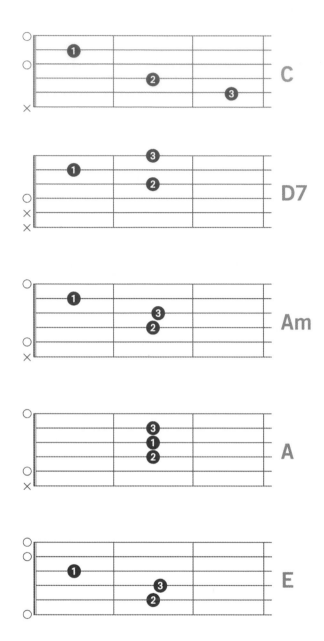

C

D7

Am

A

E

Are there more chords? Yes, but you can play thousands of songs with the chords you know. These chords are the most commonly used chords in guitar...and every future chord will be "another chord" instead of "the first chord."

TO MASTER GUITAR PLAYING YOU MUST PLAY YOUR GUITAR!*

CONGRATULATIONS!
Rhythm Is Most Important, and You've Learned a Lot of Rhythm!

THE ALTERNATE STRUM:

⊓ ∨ ⊓ ∨ ⊓ ∨ ⊓ ∨
① + ② + ③ + ④ +   etc.

‖: D   A7 | G   A7   :‖

RIFFING:

The Wild Riff

⊓   ⊓ ⊓   ⊓   ⊓ ⊓   ⊓   ⊓ ⊓
① + ② + 3 ④ + ① + ② + 3 ④ +

‖: G   G   C C | D   D   C C :‖

THE BASIC STRUM:

⊓   ⊓ ∨ ⊓   ⊓ ∨   ⊓   ⊓ ∨ ⊓   ⊓ ∨
① + ② + ③ + ④ + ① + ② + ③ + ④ +

‖: D | G   :‖

THE BEST STRUM:

⊓   ⊓ ∨   ∨ ⊓ ∨   ⊓   ⊓ ∨   ∨ ⊓ ∨
① + ② + 3 ④ + ① + ② + 3 ④ +

‖: G | C   :‖

MIXED RHYTHMS AND SPLIT MEASURES:

HERE IS THE BASIC STRUM   HERE IS THE BEST STRUM
↓   ↓
⊓   ⊓ ∨ ⊓   ⊓ ∨   ⊓   ⊓ ∨   ∨ ⊓ ∨
① + ② + ③ + ④ + ① + ② + 3 ④ +

‖: D   G | A7   :‖

HERE IS THE BEST STRUM   HERE IS THE BASIC STRUM
↓   ↓
⊓   ⊓ ∨   ∨ ⊓ ∨   ⊓   ⊓ ∨ ⊓   ⊓ ∨
① + ② + 3 ④ + ① + ② + ③ + ④ +

‖: G | C   A7   :‖

And how about all your vital habits?

GOOD GUITARISTS KNOW THAT
PLAYING IN RHYTHM IS MOST IMPORTANT!
The secret to playing great rhythm guitar is to move your hand with the beat.
Usually this means: ON the beat, strum DOWN. OFF the beat, strum UP.

Good guitarists are efficient.
LEAVE FINGERS DOWN WHENEVER POSSIBLE
—PIVOT, PIVOT, PIVOT!

USE YOUR FINGERTIP TO FRET NOTES,
ALMOST BUT NOT QUITE ON THE FRET.

STRUM EFFICIENTLY, USING REST STROKES.

WHEN CHANGING CHORDS,
MOVE THE MOST IMPORTANT FINGER FIRST.

ALWAYS PLAY THE OPTIMUM NUMBER OF
STRINGS IN A CHORD.

PERCEIVE AND REMEMBER PATTERNS IN MUSIC!

CELEBRATE! You've been a music listener. But now you are a music creator! I'm so excited for you. You know how to play guitar.

I've always loved watching and listening to other people make music. For a kid growing up in North Idaho back in my day this meant listening to the Old Time Fiddlers at the annual Locust Blossom Festival and 100% of other local events. I gotta tell you, they were pretty good!

But as much as I enjoyed listening to the old timers energetically saw away to "Orange Blossom Special" it seemed like some things were missing—things like screaming electric guitars, towering stacks of amplifiers, a haze of fog and smoke. Old Time Fiddler concerts also lacked basic health risks like unsafe mosh pits, seizure-inducing light shows. and the chance of short term hearing loss. Clearly, I needed to go to a rock concert!

Big touring rock bands rarely passed through my part of the world. But luckily, they did sometimes visit Beasley Coliseum, just 50 miles away across the border in Pullman, Washington. So my best friend Ted, his brother Jed, my brother Luke and I all saved up to see Heart. They put on an amazing show. Nancy Wilson played incredible guitar! There was a light show! There was fog! And after experiencing deafness for several days, I learned of an advanced audio safety technology called "earplugs." It was exactly what I wanted.

Years later, I had the pleasure of visiting Madison Square Garden with my two oldest kids for their first concert—Muse. There was amazing music! There were lights and fog. And I made them wear earplugs—but they did get to stay up really late. They loved it!

Then I took my youngest daughter to her first concert, Billie Eilish at Radio City Music Hall. Billie Eilish put on an wonderful, generous show. There were lights. There was fog. And my daughter had a wonderful time.

I also remember my other first concerts...the ones where we were the "stars." My first show was at Earth Day in Friendship Square Park in Moscow, Idaho. And some of the most fun I've had as a dad was being a roadie for the band my son and daughter put together in elementary school, The Neon Cows, when they played their first concert on a loading dock at a defunct carpet factory in Yonkers.

But as much fun as I've had being performed for, and performing, my greatest memories of music are informal—sharing music with others in play-alongs or jams, or picking up my guitar to feel my own joys and sorrows.

I'm so grateful to you for opening this book and playing along with it. It's such a pleasure and honor to make music together with you. We may not be in the same place or time together—but we are definitely in the same great universal song!

I have a few more songs for you. **"Therefore I Am" by Billie Eilish** reminds me of that concert with my daughter—it's a straightforward two-chord song, and since *E* and *Am* have the exact same finger shape, try to "chunk" your fingers to move them at the same time. **"Rescue Me" by Fontella Bass** was recorded in just three takes, which is a great reminder to all of us to just get going. And **"Rescue Me"** and **"Old Town Road" by Lil Nas X** both mix four major chords in the same song. **"Old Town Road"** doesn't feature a fiddle—but it does have a banjo.

THEREFORE I AM
PERFORMED BY BILLIE EILISH

Am

E

CAPO 5

Chorus

| Am | Am | E | E |

I'm not your friend,   or an-y-thing.   Damn, you think that you're the man.   I think, there-fore I am   I'm not your

| Am | Am | E | E |

friend,   or an-y-thing   Damn,   you think that you're the man.   I think, there fore I am.

Verse

| Am | Am |

Stop.   What the hell are you talk-ing a-bout?   Ha!   Get my pret-ty name out ta your mouth
talk   'bout me like   how you might know how I feel.   Top of the world, but your world is-n't real.

| E | E |

We're not the same,   with or with-out.   Don't
Your world's an i-deal.   So, go have

Pre-Chorus

| Am | Am |

fun.   I real-ly could-n't care less,   and you can give 'em my best,   but just just know,   I'm   not   your

---

CHORUS

VERSE 2
I don't want press to put your name next to mine
  we're on different lines, so I
Wanna be nice enough, they don't call my bluff
  'cause I hate to find
Articles, articles, articles
  rather you remain unremarkable (Got a lotta)
Interviews, interviews, interviews
  when they say your name, I just act confused

PRE-CHORUS

CHORUS

BRIDGE (VERSE)
I'm sorry
I don't think I caught your name
I'm sorry
I don't think I caught your name

CHORUS

RESCUE ME
PERFORMED BY FONTELLA BASS

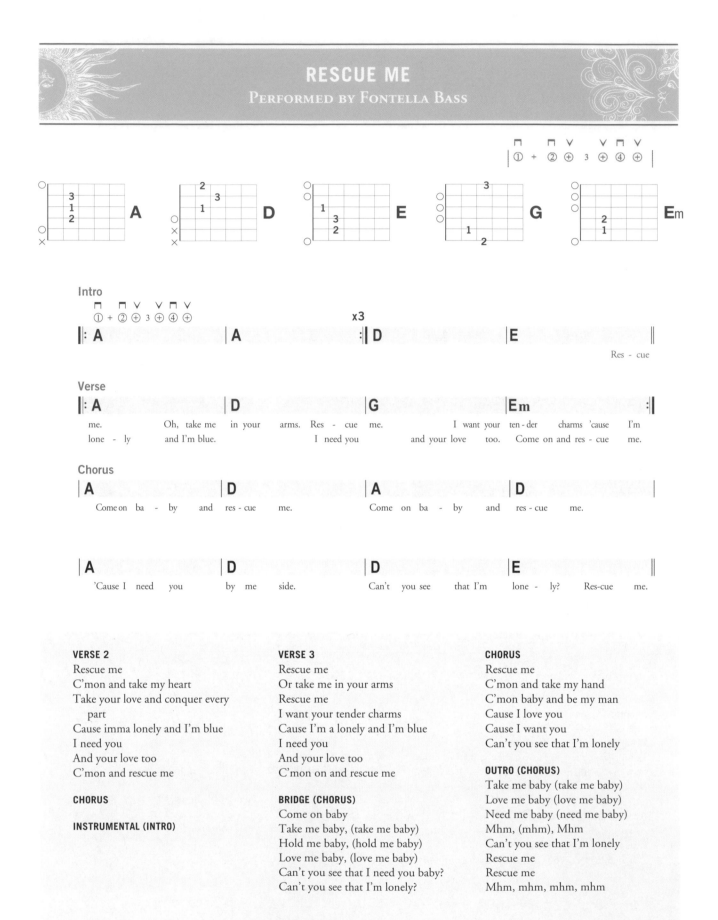

VERSE 2

Rescue me
C'mon and take my heart
Take your love and conquer every
    part
Cause imma lonely and I'm blue
I need you
And your love too
C'mon and rescue me

CHORUS

INSTRUMENTAL (INTRO)

VERSE 3

Rescue me
Or take me in your arms
Rescue me
I want your tender charms
Cause I'm a lonely and I'm blue
I need you
And your love too
C'mon on and rescue me

BRIDGE (CHORUS)

Come on baby
Take me baby, (take me baby)
Hold me baby, (hold me baby)
Love me baby, (love me baby)
Can't you see that I need you baby?
Can't you see that I'm lonely?

CHORUS

Rescue me
C'mon and take my hand
C'mon baby and be my man
Cause I love you
Cause I want you
Can't you see that I'm lonely

OUTRO (CHORUS)

Take me baby (take me baby)
Love me baby (love me baby)
Need me baby (need me baby)
Mhm, (mhm), Mhm
Can't you see that I'm lonely
Rescue me
Rescue me
Mhm, mhm, mhm, mhm

CAPO 4

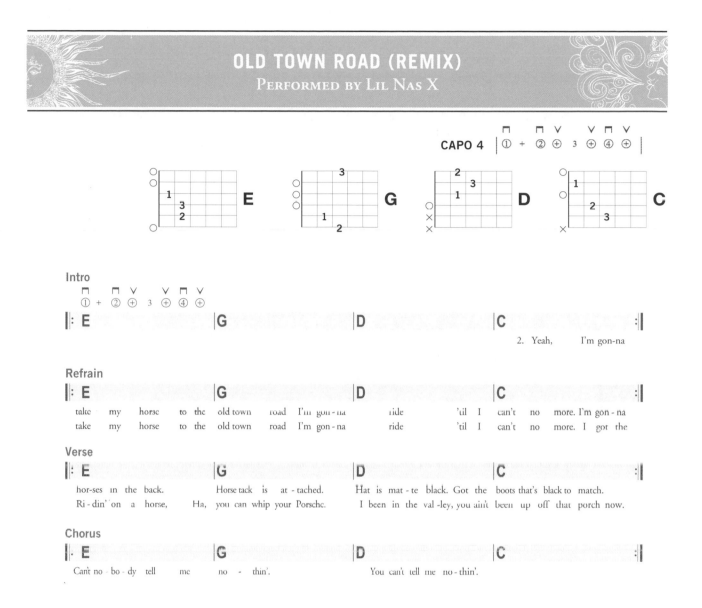

Intro

```
:|| E        |G        |D        |C        :||
```

2. Yeah,   I'm gon-na

Refrain

```
:|| E        |G        |D        |C        :||
```

take   my   horse   to the   old town   road   I'm gon-na   ride   'til   I   can't   no   more. I'm gon-na

take   my   horse   to the   old town   road   I'm gon-na   ride   'til   I   can't   no   more. I got the

Verse

```
:|| E        |G        |D        |C        :||
```

hor-ses   in the   back.   Horse tack is at-tached.   Hat is mat-te black. Got the boots that's black to match.

Ri-din' on a   horse,   Ha, you can whip your Porsche.   I been in the val-ley, you ain't been up off that porch now.

Chorus

```
:|| E        |G        |D        |C        :||
```

Can't no-bo-dy tell   me   no - thin'.   You can't tell me no-thin'.

VERSE 2

Ridin' on a tractor
Lean all in my bladder
Cheated on my baby
You can go and ask her
My life is a movie
Bull ridin' and boobies
Cowboy hat from Gucci
Wrangler on my booty

CHORUS

REFRAIN

VERSE 3

Hat down, cross town, livin' like a rockstar
Spent a lot of money on my brand new guitar
Baby's got a habit: diamond rings and Fendi sports bras
Ridin' down Rodeo in my Maserati sports car
Got no stress, I've been through all that
I'm like a Marlboro Man so I kick on back
Wish I could roll on back to that old town road
I wanna ride 'til I can't no more

OUTRO (REFRAIN)

TO PRACTICE GUITAR OR ANYTHING SUCCESSFULLY:

✓ Practice accurately. *Festina Lente* ("hurry slowly"). When you practice guitar, practice accurately to create correct patterns in your mind and body.

✓ Practice guitar regularly!

> *The heights by great men reached and kept,*
> *Were not attained by sudden flight.*
> *But they, while their companions slept,*
> *Were toiling upwards in the night.*
>
> —*H.W. Longfellow*

✓ Practice effectively. "If something is worth doing, it is worth doing well." Pay attention to what you are doing.

Dear NYC Guitar School Student—

Congratulations on completing Guitar for Absolute Beginners at New York City Guitar School. In order to finish this class, you've needed to fulfill a commitment to yourself to attend class and to practice. This is a big accomplishment as a guitar player and as a human.

In this class you learned the fundamental habits, chords and rhythms of a good guitar player. You can build on this knowledge over a lifetime of playing. If you would like more formal study we would be privileged to continue helping you in your progress. The next class, Guitar for Near Beginners, covers the fundamentals of expression and tone, as well as adding more rhythms, chords and songs.

Thank you for taking a class at New York City Guitar School. Your teacher, our entire staff and I appreciate the opportunity to be part of your life.

Congratulations on deciding to PLAY GUITAR!

Sincerely,

Dan Emery
Founder, New York City Guitar School

ACKNOWLEDGEMENTS

In 2004, New York City Guitar School consisted of a single room in the Recording and Rehearsal Arts Building on West 30th Street in Manhattan. One door led to the offices of four other businesses. The other led to a shared bathroom. As my students and I moved our guitars aside to allow yet another person to use the facilities, I did not imagine that eighteen years later New York City Guitar School would have over forty teachers and twenty classrooms in three locations in Manhattan, Brooklyn and Queens, or that thousands of students in New York and around the world would learn to play guitar using the curriculum you now hold in your hands. This would not have happened without the support, involvement and encouragement of hundreds of people.

The heart of a great guitar school is great teachers. Lenny Molotov, Suke Cerulo, Hector Marin, Vinnie DeMasi, Shane Chapman, Jaime Garamella, Tia Vincent-Clark, Aki Ishiguro and Michelangelo Quirinale were some of our first teachers, and are all still teaching spectacular lessons here today. I thank them for forming the core of the most student-centered guitar faculty in America, and for improving this guitar manual by letting me know what did and did not work for their students.

The progress of the book has been inseparable from the development of New York City Guitar School itself, which would not have been possible without the enthusiasm, dedication and leadership of my business partner Jen Elliott. Current and past members of our leadership team, including Martin Jacobs, Rob Adler, Madeline Johnson, Subrina Torres and Ivan Orellana, helped many nervous first time students successfully start their guitar career while managing complicated teacher schedules and physical locations. Samoa Jodha, our long-time artist and designer in residence, designed and installed beautiful walls, doors and art installations and helped create a nourishing and loving community. Elaine Chu has kept our books ever since her little girls were taking lessons here (they're both out of college now!) And Shane Chapman launched and managed our online curriculum as well as teaching and managing varied courses and endeavors over the years.

Vinnie DeMasi generously read and advised me on the material. He also did much of the research on song progressions which you'll see at the end of each lesson, edited the most recent version of the book, and with his permission I've kept some of his text and jokes intact, especially at the end of lessons 2, 3, 7 and 8. Samoa Jodha designed the photo spreads, including just some of the thousands of photos she's taken of our community. Work-study student April Koester typed the entire manual three times. Alia Madden (www.evilkid.com) created many of the striking images in the manual. The patient and gifted Chika Azuma did the amazing book design (for this and many other NYC Guitar School books!). Suzanne Bilyeu edited the first edition of the book, improving it dramatically despite removing hundreds of my precious exclamation points!! Rob Adler coordinated all of the above, as well as arranging all the songs—and keeping me on track. Brittany McCorriston carefully made final edits on the text and songs. A special thanks to Jeff Schroedl and the Hal Leonard Corporation for publishing this book complete with so many wonderful licensed songs.

The lion's share of the credit goes to the amazing New York City Guitar School Students. Early students Rita Caliendo, Nelson Cheung, Mary Ghiorzi, Gerry Borrell and especially Eric Scott encouraged me to have a larger vision of the course. Since then hundreds of students have taken a moment in the lounge, elevator or hallways to say what they liked and disliked about the course. Their support has carried me through days both fair and foul. I can't believe my good fortune to be so constantly surrounded by such wonderful and inspiring people.

Finally, thank you to my wife, Miriam, for accompanying me and supporting me in this rather incredible journey of life and music.

Dan

WANT MORE?

Join *New York City Guitar School* in NYC or online worldwide at
NYCGuitarSchool.com

For more copies of this and other books,
visit HalLeonard.com or NYCGuitarSchool.com/books.
Contact or follow us at info@NYCGuitarSchool.com,
@nycguitarschool or call 646-485-7244.

CANDID PHOTO OF THE AUTHOR, DAN EMERY
Here I am with the tools of my trade—guitar and smile—
in the guitar school lounge on West 30th Street in
Manhattan. I really enjoy teaching guitar.